*Essays on*

# Inclusive
# Stakeholding

Joo
Eri

Conrad Yun

Published by
*Yun Family Foundation*

Copyright (c) 2019 Joon Yun, Eric Yun & Conrad Yun.

Paperback ISBN: 978-1-949709-84-1

eBook ISBN: 978-1-949709-85-8

# Table of Contents

## Related Essays                                                      99

# Foreword

One thing we can do is leave stories. Many of us also leave our genes, which is nature's way of leaving better versions of ourselves. Stories shape how we do that, not only through our lives, but across space and time. Stories live a life of their own.

The essays in this anthology, *Inclusive Stakeholding*, are just that. They aren't meant to serve a particular purpose. They were written to exist for as long as they are meant to, for as long as they do.

That's not to say a reader might not take away some meaning or purpose from these stories. A person putting their story down in the year 2019 might mean it one way, while a person reading it in the year 9102 might read it another way. These stories might even provide a sense of clarity about the world or inspire action.

But above all, these stories were written to make the same sense before and after all the revolutions, all the transformations, all future comings and goings. They were written to outlast all the jubilation and all the tears.

These stories were written to live a life of their own.

# Brief and Incomplete History of the World

*A speech delivered at the United Nations headquarters
in New York City on the 50th anniversary of the lunar
landing on July 20, 2019*

Hi everyone. I'm Eric Yun, and I am honored to be here with all of you at the United Nations on this 50th anniversary of the fulfillment of President Kennedy's lunar mission. I'm here to tell you a new story, a story about history and about a new kind of mission to bring the world together.

Once upon a time, "home" was our kin village. There was mom, dad, siblings, as well as cousins, aunts, and uncles. Kin is the root of kindness, and we took care of each other according to our degrees of relatedness—a trait biologists call inclusive fitness. We were fed, informed, and governed by those who had our best interests at heart. Genetically speaking, people own 50% founder's stock in their children, 25% in their grandkids and cousins, and so on.

Today, we rely much more on strangers who have an incentive to put their own interests ahead of ours. When those entrusted to serve us don't have kin skin in the game, unfortunate things can happen. Fake news, fake foods, fake politicians all result from the same underlying cause: low genetic alignment.

Furthermore, when this malalignment is combined with competition, a "race to the bottom line" ensues. If we force one media company to use less clickbait, for example, another will use more to gain market share. If we force one food company to use less sugar, another will use more to fill the void. In a way, the Kardashian culture and high-fructose corn syrup are the same phenomenon—the inevitable outcome of a race to the bottom line, where malalignment meets capitalism.

But it's not just institutions versus people. It's also people against each other. Deep fractures seem to appear daily along every tribal element of human identity. As in some apocalyptic action movies, we hardly know where to step in our day-to-day conversations for fear of falling into some crevasse of bubbling hate that has just opened up.

The tragedy is that these tribal hurrahs might prove as phony as SPAM when it first appeared as a poor replacement for meat, and later, as an even worse replacement for a friend's handwritten letter. If loyalty is a fleeting and tradable commodity, is it still loyalty? Without the kin skin in the game that existed in our original tribes, true loyalty within today's "tribes" will remain as elusive as it has been since the beginning of the human diaspora a hundred thousand years ago. Rather than healing the wounds of alienation, today's tribalism throws salt in them. That's hardly the type of future anyone would dream of, yet an everyone-for-themselves nightmare is exactly what looms as the sun sets on this brief and remarkable interlude known as human history.

This alienation has been going on far longer than you might think. Looking back, world history as we know it has largely been a story of how family values failed to scale as humans globalized. When kingship replaced kinship, sovereigns began ruling over instead of on behalf of their people. Ancient republics created to counter these abuses also collapsed, usually due to self-dealing. As republics and empires everywhere collapsed under the burden of self-interested corruption, it was perhaps inevitable that the story of a deity who gave his only son to the world emerged to counter the story of kings who gave the world to their sons. But this story also gave way to the same old story of institutional corruption until Martin Luther's revolution in 1517.

Around that time, the idea of a joint-stock company was born. This powerful idea aligned stakeholders the way genes once did for kin tribes. But these companies did not include their workers or people in distant lands as stakeholders, which led to imperialism, colonialism, and the exacerbation of abusive working conditions brought on by the industrial revolution. Against this backdrop, firms that gave stock to their workers was a stunning innovation that made Silicon Valley the entrepreneurial juggernaut it is today. On the other hand, Silicon Valley did not include users as stakeholders, which is resulting in yet another round of upheavals today.

These examples demonstrate a recurring theme: unless first-order alignment issues are addressed, whack-a-mole solutions to second-order problems will only create new ones. Pete Townshend anthemized this Sisyphean hell of revolutions in "Won't Get Fooled Again": the new boss is often the same old boss.

A group of excluded stakeholders has been paying the price ever since we left the kin-skin-in-the-game era of human evolution—the price of tyranny, slavery, nepotism, nationalism, nativism, imperialism, colonialism, racism, pollution, extractive capitalism, corruption, alienation, loneliness, and inequality. The good news is that the solution is hiding in plain sight. We're at that "tap your heels together three times", when we finally realize that we've had the power to change our story all along. Humanity's natural condition is not independence but inter-dependence, and the arc of human history has been nothing more than our failure to replace the inclusive fitness of the kin village with the inclusive stakeholding of the global village. The struggle for inclusive stakeholding is the First Principle of Humanity, from which can be derived not only historical understanding but a path to building a better future for everyone. This is very doable.

To begin doing this, our family is launching the Grand Challenge on Inclusive Stakeholding, a social innovation competition intended to nurture new types of social, political, and economic institutions in which all people win as all stake-holders win—including those who don't have a voice, such as the children of the future. I will offer some examples.

Imagine health insurers being rewarded based on people's healthcare savings ten years down the road. If a proportion of the health savings of that patient over ten years accrues to the original insurer, then the insurer becomes an inves-tor-stakeholder in the client's health, which motivates them to encourage preventive health measures. Or, imagine teachers being rewarded in token amounts on the blockchain that are based on their students' contributions to the world ten years down the road. The pupils' success would lift up all their prior teachers. Instead of universal basic income, imagine universal basic stakeholding, where we all have a stake in one another's future.

In the olden days, warring kingdoms would make peace by marrying off their kids to create interdependence and kin skin in the game. Today we can build networks of interdependent stakeholders to create a social economy, as Facebook did for social media but much, much bigger. I'm sure each of you can think of many more possibilities, and we are all aligned with the success of one another's ideas. Whereas malalignment with competition is a race to the bottom, alignment with competition is a race to the top.

The stakes have never been higher. We live today in a highly interconnected world and our futures are irrevocably intertwined as never before, both as individuals and as nations. From ecological impact to humanitarian crises to space exploration, we all have a stake in the risks and opportunities arising across the planet. Embracing inclusive stakeholding is our final frontier, and our future depends on it.

Like Captain Neil Armstrong, I dream of things that fly and fly far. Instead of a world where history is written by the victors, I dream of a world where history is made by helping others win. If we succeed in this vision for humanity, our transformative journey from the kin village to the global village will be complete. I know that sounds crazy, but if President Kennedy were here today, he would ask us to aim beyond the moon. He would ask us to aim for the stars. I hope you will join me in this new mission. I wish you all good luck, and Godspeed.

# First Principle of Humanity: The Principle of Inclusive Stakeholding

The First Principle of Humanity is Inclusive Stakeholding: assigning a stake to others in the widest sense, including those who currently don't have a voice, and our future children. From this First Principle, large-scale human history can be derived and a better future for all can be imagined.

Evolution selected our social instincts to align with kin tribes. For the longest time, it probably was difficult for early humans *to avoid* living in kin tribes. The benefit of kin-based living was too high, as was the cost of avoiding it. That was our Eden—our social nirvana of time immemorial.

In that cradle of human evolution, there was less need for consciousness. Follow your instincts and things worked out. It might be no accident, then, that the kin tribe era left us no record. Perhaps life for them just *was*.

But somewhere along the way, humans harnessed the Promethean Fire and learned to make tools. That knowledge uprooted humans from their kin tribes and the era of social entropy began. As lineages arborized, kinship thinned. The hive became a house divided. Descendants battled and were banished to a life of wandering. The dispersion and diasporas hit their planetary limits and merged into melting pots.

Looking back, the journey to now has been mostly a beautiful one. But the human experience over the past ten thousand years has also brought an ever-increasing awareness of the existence of good and bad, expressed through the service or disservice of others, either according to, or in spite of, Hamilton's rule.

The battle between these forces has been as dramatic as the prehistoric kin tribe era was undramatic. Every collision between kin-based societies and societies built on competition—for example when the Native Americans met Europeans—resulted in the annihilation of the former due to advanced weaponry possessed by cultures with commodification. But over longer cycle times, even the latter category of cultures built on commodification also imploded. Thus, as per Ibn Khaldun's *Asabiyyah*, all civilizations began to rise and fall. Strange things started to happen regularly. It began to be worthwhile to observe, contemplate, and act in profoundly new ways.

But by and large, we've had to learn by trial and error. Ideas that seemed good to the parade of conquerors, revolutionaries, and social reformers that have disproportionately shaped our collective history delivered disappointing—if not downright destructive—results. Yet, we were never quite sure why. Even though we've made great progress in improving our material existence, the rising tide that has buoyed us materially has also unmoored us spiritually. Too many parts of the human experience feel soulless. For the vast majority of people alive today, the price of progress has been a loss of a sense of belonging that were the anchors of human experience for most of the history of our species. This cost has been significant—and, even more to the point, one we've not even begun to seriously recognize or address.

We are genetically wired for the kin tribe era, but we no longer live as such. That's a first-order problem that continues to spawn second- and third-order issues in a degenerating cascade. So, the time has come to return to our roots. It's time to restart at year zero.

Just as Caesar had no idea that future historians would count the calendar years of his reign in a backwards regression to zero, just as every person basking in the sunlight a thousand years ago was unaware that Petrarch would later label their era the Dark Ages, and just as everyone once thought the earth was bigger than the sun, we today are blind to the possibility that our journey forward has been a journey homeward.

We left our kin village. We envisioned our role as the hero that would slay the beast. We instead got cast in the role of the villain by an unconditionally loving hero. It turned out that these stock archetypes are the farthest things from the truth. There never was a beast to slay or a hero to worship. The same actor has been behind all the roles. Us.

The story we are telling is that our lives—all of our lives—are best served by encompassing some mix of both modes of living. Enlightened self-interest as a social code works best when we also have greater alignment and vested interest in each other's lives. The change that *will* matter most is to update the bioalgorithms of inclusive fitness in the tribal era with the social algorithms of inclusive stakeholding in the global era.

That's because, seen through a wider lens, human history is a story of how kin skin in the game has scaled poorly as the operating algorithm of human sociality in the global era. That is an evolutionary lag error of epic proportions—but one that is eminently addressable. The Grand Challenge on Inclusive Stakeholding, a social innovation competition intended to reimagine our social, political, and economic institutions through alignment of interests and goal congruence, is part of a larger roadmap to help us find our way home. If we succeed, our transformative journey from the kin village to the global village will be complete. It turns out that our hero's journey was not to pursue our own, but to steward each other's journey homeward. We will return not as heroes, nor as the prodigal sons and daughters, but as both. The two sets of footprints we leave in the wilderness will be one set, not because one is carrying the other, but because we're headed home together again.

# The Inevitability of Religion, the Kardashians, and Larry Harvey

Picture this. In the historical drama film *Gladiator,* which depicted the Roman Empire as it was heading toward collapse, Maximus, the blood sport's rising star who was challenging the corruption of a philistine society, does a product endorsement.

Between death matches.

For olive oil.

If you think that sounds too absurd, even for a movie about a circus-like era of human history, so did the movie's producers. They deleted this scene from the script because they thought the idea of a gladiator doing commercial endorsements detracted from the realistic feel of the story.[1]

Yet the reality is that gladiators in Ancient Rome did, in fact, use their celebrity to endorse products.[2] The frescos and graffiti of the gladiator era suggest that people back then trusted the purchase advice of their superstar heroes just as they do today.

1. See Griffin, Joshua, "Not Such a Wonderful Life: A Look at History in Gladiator," IGN, January 13, 2019, https://www.ign.com/articles/2000/02/10/not-such-a-wonderful-life-a-look-at-history-in-gladiator.
2. See Cyrino, Monica S. "Gladiator and Contemporary American Society," in Gladiator: Film and History, ed. Martin M. Winkler (Oxford, UK: Blackwell, 2004), 124-49, http://faculty.uml.edu/ethan_spanier/teaching/documents/cyrinogaldiator.pdf.

There is a powerful scene in the movie when young Lucius approaches Maximus as the latter is about to enter the arena.[3] The poignant moment portrays the influence celebrity athletes wield over children who idolize them. The scene is not dissimilar to that depicted in one of the most successful product endorsements of all-time: Coke's campaign in which a wounded Mean Joe Greene is offered a Coke in the tunnel of an arena by a wide-eyed young fanboy, who is thanked with a smile.[4]

In the prehistoric kin tribe era, our larger-than-life role models would have been our aunts and uncles or even our parents. This familial sense is evoked in the Lucius-Maximus scene in *Gladiator*, as Lucius is fatherless, and Maximus's own son has been murdered. From an inclusive fitness perspective, idolizing and modeling our lives after the celebrities in our prehistoric kin tribe and trusting the ideas and products they endorsed would have served us well. In other words, evolution selected for an innate tendency to trust the endorsements of our avuncular (uncle) and materteral (aunt) heroes.

The authors of this book are members of a kin tribe. We live within five minutes of each other. The avuncular and materteral influences of our tribal past have disappeared from our daily lives and been replaced by stand-in pseudo-uncles and pseudo-aunts who don't have kin skin in the game. Modern day celebrities and so-called heroes have an incentive to self-deal and exploit their worshipers for personal gain through extractive capitalism.

Just as Coke made a lot of money at the expense of children who reflexively and almost unavoidably followed their genetic scripting, trusting the ideas and products that modern celebrities endorse is an evolutionary maladaptation.

Seen from a higher perch, this dynamic is nefarious. Once upon a time, our mother—or other kin with a vested in interest in our success—nurtured us. Now we interface with counterparties with no kin skin in the game—the ever-present self-dealing archetype in *Cinderella, Snow White,* and other folklore tales: the evil stepmother.[5]

---

3. See https://getyarn.io/yarn-clip/20e01580-7afe-4eb5-8fef-5f6e61e65ba0.
4. See "Mean" Joe Greene Coca-Cola Classic ad, 1979, https://www.youtube.com/watch?v=xffOCZYX6F8.
5. See https://en.wikipedia.org/wiki/Stepmother.

In *Interdependent Capitalism*, our previous volume, we explored how, without kin skin in the game to deter self-dealing, natural inclinations and free markets inevitably precipitate a race to the bottom line that maximizes commodification (i.e., creating things for their trading value). This mass production of nothing-is-quite-what-it-seems outcomes is what makes touristy destinations feel alienating, spec homes feel cheap, and, frankly, virtually every frontier of human experience feel soulless.

Earlier we mentioned that religion and the Kardashians were inevitable consequences of extractive governance and extractive capitalism, which emerged when kin skin in the game failed to scale during globalization. The same process inevitably also produced Larry Harvey, the founder of Burning Man—a rebellion against cultural commodification—no matter how many times we rerun this simulation called civilization.

Seen through a wider lens—without kin skin in the game to deter individual self-dealing—the evolutionary race to commodify selects extractive behaviors over good behaviors until only the former survive as self-expanding, self-serving institutions. By treating the symptoms but not the causes of aging, for example, our health system creates old people who need more healthcare, creating a vicious cycle. Food, media, and tech industries are growing through cycles of addiction. Big banks and big government have already become too big to fail.

The bottom line is this. When there's alignment of interest, competition selects what's best for the group. When there isn't goal congruence, competition selects for power. Here we are in 2019 at the feet of self-expanding beasts everywhere that seem as undefeatable as cancer.

# The Story of Our Nature and the Nature of Our Stories

Humanity is trapped in a cycle.

The institutions we built to attack self-expanding beasts in one era became the self-expanding beasts of the next. Along the way, we have made great strides in the collective quality of life on the planet, yet there is growing dread about where the world is headed.

To step out of this cycle, we've made the case that the change that will matter most is rebuilding our institutions through the Principle of Inclusive Stakeholding, where people win as others win.

But we can do even better.

Whether through kin skin in the game or inclusive stakeholding, kindness can be induced through secondary gain—that's just the story of our nature. Yet humans also display kindness for kindness' sake, even in the absence of incentives.

In the battle to overcome our default programming of following incentives—and to inspire us to show more kindness as agents of mercy rather than as mercenaries—there is a powerful secret weapon: stories.

Picture the difference between someone holding the door for another person for a tip versus someone holding the door for the sake of holding the door. The former is the commodification of kindness—done for the trading value. The latter is the decommodification of kindness—kindness for itself. One might argue that the outcome is the same either way and that only the experience differs. On the other hand, one might argue that the difference in experience is everything.

We know that people are more than capable of doing the right thing even without incentives, if they are acculturated to do so. We also know that people do the right thing even in the absence of such acculturation.

This is where stories—through acculturation—can make a difference.

––––––––––––

The nature of our stories, however, has fundamentally changed. Over the course of human evolution, the same phenomenon that affected the evolution of human social systems affected the evolution of stories. As we became more mobile and our vested interest in each other declined, stories shifted from serving the interest of the kin hive to serving the interests of the storyteller. People began to sell—instead of tell—stories. Think of every Instagram post ever.

In the process, the storytelling market became the biggest self-expanding beast of all.

In the context of commodification, the natural dynamic of the marketplace for stories is a race to the bottom: whatever sells best at the time. The co-evolution of stories, storytellers, and story-listeners selects for the high-fructose corn syrup of stories and storytellers, hijacking the human storytelling/story-listening neural pathways to serve themselves. In a way, stories themselves become self-expanding superorganisms—or memetic beasts. Commodified stories are pouring in, sweeping up children and adults—tranquilized by "feel good" hooks and other appealing devices—into the belly of the beast.

The story industry has optimized these hooks to maximize attention, which in and of itself is not evil. But the intention to use these hooks to serve their own interests at the expense of the people is the nefarious force. Be wary of such self-dealing storytellers, their accomplices, and their industries: entertainment, publishing, podcasts, media, speaker series, etc.

But most of all, be wary of the stories themselves as they get commodified.

For example, advocacy means speaking up for others, but schools now teach *self-advocacy*. Yet the more each person self-advocates, the more everyone has to yell ever louder to be the loudest chick in the nest—that's a race to the bottom.

Eventually, it becomes about the screaming itself. Victimhood and self-righteous marches ensue.

Many other words have been similarly hijacked to serve storytellers. *Mindfulness* used to mean being mindful of others, but now it is part of a personal-enrichment movement.[6] Alumni office means development, and development means fundraising. Free trade means special interests, and special interests means self-interest. Concession stand means rip-off stand, and "all natural" means, well, nothing.

It is our nature to nurture, but the story market, instead, picked more marketable versions of the truth by Thomas Paine and Jean-Jacques Rousseau who sold stories that it is our nature to be independent. Whether it's declaring independence from a king that promised to take care of us or writing a bill of individual rights, these stories address the symptoms, and not the root cause of these issues—which is our abdication of responsibility to each other. When we used to take responsibility for each other, there was no reason to talk about self-reliance, a field Ralph Waldo Emerson launched in 1841.[7]

Why, by the way, are we still celebrating our divorce from Britain when we're living together? Shouldn't we be writing up the declaration of interdependence?

Capitalists think socialists extract, and socialists think capitalists extract. And then you have Ayn Rand, who thinks all institutions extract. But who will write the story truth that the lack of skin in the game is what makes them all extract? Instead, Karl Marx, Adam Smith, and Charles Dickens eloquently described cultural symptoms as if they were causes. How about the story that capitalism and socialism might *both* work with proper stakeholding?

But no category better epitomizes the self-expanding nature of commodified stories than the self-help movement. In the book marketplace, imagine trying to sell a book about being mindful of others, advocating for others, and taking responsibility for others. Such books (except for religious books) would find a

6. See Yun, Jeremy, Remarks Delivered at the 2017 Purpose Awards (Kindle version), https://www.amazon.com/Remarks-Delivered-2017-Purpose-Awards-ebook/dp/B0763JW4YH/.
7. See Emerson, Ralph Waldo, "Self-Reliance," https://en.wikipedia.org/wiki/Self-Reliance.

limited audience, so authors tend not to write them. Such stories do exist, among the countless stories in the memesphere, but those tend not to be the stories that attract commercial demand, so the publishers tend not to publish them.

What do sell—the literary litter that self-promoting authors and publishers are willing to create—are self-help books. Next time you go to a bookstore, marvel at how large the self-help section is and how much it has grown during your lifetime. Compare it to the size of the "help others" section of the bookstore.

"What 'help others' section?" you might well ask.

Exactly.

Help is a concept that used to involve a second person, until George Combe inaugurated the self-help movement in 1829.[8] Love, like compassion, is something we bestow on others, but love stories have been hijacked and mutated into stories about loving oneself and having self-compassion. These methods treat the symptoms of mutual alienation and loneliness but not the underlying causes. Who will write the truth—that the "self" movement *is* the cause of mutual alienation and loneliness? No wonder that, despite being connected to more people than ever, many of us feel more alienated and alone than ever.

Which brings us to the so-called hero's journey. One could make the case that the sum total of all the heroes' journeys in the world have gotten us to exactly where we are as a society today. What if our obsession with being the hero, slaying the beast, and being transformed is a central contributor to our current dystopia? What if our obsession with our *own* journey, heroic or otherwise, is itself a self-expanding beast of the type we described above?

People have been memetically primed to buy all of these books. The publishing industry is more than happy to profit from selling into this memetic channel, thereby expanding its own balance sheet and market power. Self-promotion becomes the engine that feeds itself through the publishing ecosystem.[9] In the competitive race to the bottom, the system selects for the high-fructose corn syrup version of every story in order to sell more books.

---

8. See https://en.wikipedia.org/wiki/Self-help.
9. The system selects for fake stories with fake relevance for the reader.

The "kryptonite" needed to fight these beasts is the same throughout this book: the energy of the beast against itself—the Aikido Principle—which, in this case, means to use the incentive prize model to cure the perverse incentives. This process instantiates our core belief that was articulated in *Interdependent Capitalism*—that there is no separation of hero and beast, and that the hero's journey is to steward the journeys of others. In other words, Grendel was never a beast: thus, it is our duty is to steward Grendel's journey to return as the hero.

In practical terms, this means that our storytelling industry is our best ally to transform our current stories to their decommodified forms. It is with great pleasure, then, for us to sponsor the Grand Challenge on Stories with the aim of surfacing stories that will best serve the interests of the people, leveraging everything we have learned about storytelling.

We are specifically looking for updated versions of the following pieces of work, written in a way that reflects a deep understanding of the First Principle of Humanity: Plato's *The Republic*, Thomas Paine's *Common Sense*, Jean-Jacques Rousseau's *The Social Contract*, Adam Smith's *The Wealth of Nations*, Karl Marx *Das Kapital*, and Ayn Rand's *The Fountainhead*. We are also seeking updated copies of the Declaration of Interdependence and the Bill of Responsibilities. But we will consider the rewrite of any great work that incorporates the First Principle of Humanity.

Will we truly be able to put the genie back in the bottle and everything back into Pandora's jar? We are rather optimistic that the world is on the brink of an inclusive stakeholding transformation, but in the free market for stories, it is easier to sell the story that this is impossible, than to tell the story that it is not only possible, but about to happen.

However, every Yang leads to another Yin, and every action causes a reaction. No matter how we render the future with the best of our intentions, the world will never lack the need for the next generation of stewards to shore up issues left behind by their predecessors. Inclusive stakeholding may be a salve for the panoply of extractive behaviors, but no matter how much we try to do our best, it is inevitable that a new system of victors and victims will arise. The Yin and Yang, the Hegelian dialectic, the path of the serpent—the shape of every form of energy—ensures there will always be a new direction for human endeavor.

It is with this sobering perspective in mind we leave behind the following thought: let's leave behind a library of uncommodified foundational stories—fairy tales of tomorrow that serve the interests of the people—that will be just as relevant into the indefinite future as they were to our primordial ancestors a long, long time ago.

# Kin Diaspora, Social Entropy, and Relationship Liquidity

Family branches inexorably become estranged over the generations. Put differently, a house divides, and the divided houses keep dividing. The genetic alignment of the original house gets increasingly diluted with each generation, but each new kin hive is internally just as closely aligned genetically as was the original hive.[10] The lineages of Cain and Abel in the biblical narrative were never as genetically close as the brothers themselves. Kin altruism is reborn with every new hive, but competition between hives grows over the generations as genetic alignment disappears.

The division, dispersal, and genetic fragmentation of kin tribes are features of social evolution, not bugs. They promote diversity, intergroup competition, and memetic parallax—that is, the human tendency to see better when offered multiple vantage points (to be discussed later). They also help maintain a self-regulated balance between cooperative and competitive instincts in the lineage network. The central house might have stayed put while new branches migrated to new territories. This balance of ingroup attractive forces and outgroup repulsive forces, when viewed at scale, helped maintain the kin hive structure as mass human migration took hold during the prehistoric age.[11] The human diaspora was under way.

---

10. The resulting structure is fractal in nature, with each genealogical level replicating the proximity of relationships that exist at the next higher order.
11. See https://en.wikipedia.org/wiki/Human_migration.

Two things happened subsequently that warrant mention.

First, human dispersal began to reach geographic limits. As humans started to fill various geographic niches around the planet, collisions between tribes with little genetic alignment became more frequent and relative strangers were forced to contend with one another.

Second, humans acquired the so-called Promethean Fire[12]—the knowledge and tools that enabled them to shape their own future. When humans began harnessing energy, early on through horses and later through hydrocarbons, it enabled breathtaking progress, but it also increased the probability that competing tribes with little genetic alignment would collide with each other.

The increasing collision of tribes had profound effects, which to a significant extent were bloody. The diaspora that had started in humanity's cradle began to eat itself, and the slaughter of strangers and hegemony over the vanquished became all too common. On the other hand, trading of ideas and goods also began to flourish.

Energy increases the entropy of systems, and social entropy is no different. As human social systems harnessed energy, relationship liquidity—defined as the average number of people connected to a particular person and the potential number of transactions among them—vastly increased. There are many beneficial aspects to having a higher number of interpersonal interactions, as having access to more people can increase the probability of finding better partners, in life and in business.

Over time, as converging cultures blended into melting pots, unprecedented levels of prosperity ensued. To be sure, in addition to the propulsive forces of kin dispersal, a different force—the centripetal force of migration toward greener pastures of opportunity—also drew us away from each other and into agglomerative forces of human connection, such as cities. As Jane Jacobs chronicled in her work, *The Economy of Cities,* the diversity of people who gathered in the world's first cities came with a diversity of ideas. This dynamic set into motion a positive

---

12. See https://en.wikipedia.org/wiki/Prometheus.

feedback of city inventiveness and city growth that propelled humanity from the Iron Age through the Space Age and to the present day.

Fast forward to today, the social mobility enabled by innovations in technology, communication, and transportation has dramatically increased the liquidity of our relationships. Some of the hard-wired social traits that we inherited from our tribally-minded ancestors have been rendered maladaptive by evolutionary dislocation and are no longer properly suited to handle modern relationship dynamics.

Our attraction to new social opportunities was shaped when such opportunities were far more limited than they are today. Not unlike our attraction to sweet, fatty, and salty foods, little selection pressure existed in the old world for evolving upper limits on our attractions for new social opportunities. But does a tendency to be intrigued by new social opportunities make us happier people in a world where access to new opportunities is virtually limitless?

Whereas our prehistoric tribal predecessors may have had access to a limited set of potential mates, friends, and colleagues, humans today can choose from a vast inventory of possible relationships in our mobile society and even meet distant partners through the internet. There are many beneficial aspects to rising number of related transactions. Access to more people, in life and in business, can increase the probability of finding better partners. On the other hand, rising relationship liquidity and transactions have resulted in higher quantity but the lower average quality of human relationships. Furthermore, the cost of forsaking existing relationships for new ones has declined. In just the last couple of generations alone, divorce rates and job change rates have skyrocketed.

From a Darwinian perspective, agency risk today is probably much higher than our social brains were evolved to detect since the human tendency to trust counterparties was wired during the tribal era when there was a high degree of genetic alignment. A significant portion of interactions today is with non-relative individuals. This misalignment of interests increases the incentives for exploitation, and such violators of trust have more opportunities to start new relationships than ever before, thereby reducing the cost of being detected.

Indeed, agency abuse is prevalent in modern life. Corporate and political leaders are accused of enriching themselves at the expense of shareholders and citizens. Doctors are criticized for offering treatments that enrich themselves at the expense of making the best decision for their patients. The weak commitment of agents to principles can be seen as an outcome of low alignment.

Aligning interests as much as possible in human relationships may be the best way to adjust for the Darwinian maladaptation of our social brain in this era of vast relationship liquidity.

# Solidarity to "Solitarity"

Solidarity is the unity of a group based on common interests, objectives, standards, and sympathies.[13] It refers to the social ties that bind people as one.[14] Solitarity, on the other hand, is the state of being alone.[15] The two words are antonyms that together help explain the existence of an individual's concurrent and often competing interests and values at any moment in time: the feeling of wanting to have your cake and eat it too. Together they help us understand the path of history—evolutionarily, socially, and culturally—that humans have been on throughout time.

The study of social systems often has assumed that evolution proceeds from a solitary state to a social one, but recent phylogenetic studies of bees contradict this assumption.[16] In the evolution of social systems, descendants of an altruistic eusocial group can evolve back to solitary behavior once again—a phenomenon known as a reversal to solitarity, or secondary solitarity.[17] Eusociality in bees is thought to have evolved at least four times, and reversal of a species to solitarity is thought to have occurred at least nine separate times.[18] [19] It's possible that humans are headed to becoming the tenth known example of a species in the animal kingdom that evolved from a social system of solidarity to one of solitarity.

13. See https://www.merriam-webster.com/dictionary/solidarity.
14. See https://en.wikipedia.org/wiki/Solidarity.
15. See https://en.wikipedia.org/wiki/Eusociality.
16. See Wcislo, William T., and Bryan N. Danforth, "Secondarily Solitary: The Evolutionary Loss of Social Behavior," Trends in Ecology & Evolution 12 no. 12 (1997): 468-474, https://www.sciencedirect.com/science/article/pii/S0169534797011981.
17. See Wcislo and Danforth, "Secondarily Solitary," https://www.sciencedirect.com/science/article/pii/S0169534797011981.
18. Gadagkar, R., "And Now... Eusocial Thrips!" Current Science 64 (1993): 215-216; Michener, C. D., "Comparative Social Behavior of Bees," Annual Review of Entomology 14 (1969): 299-342.
19. See Wcislo and Danforth, "Secondarily Solitary," https://www.sciencedirect.com/science/article/pii/S0169534797011981; https://en.wikipedia.org/wiki/Eusociality#Reversal_to_solitarity.

The evolutionary lag error between modern cultural evolution and our biological factory settings—a fundamental evolutionary maladaptation—has produced millennia of dysfunction in the operating-system level of human society, where individual self-interest trumps interpersonal interests. As noted in prior essays, the response at this level has been awkward at best and self-destructive at worst.

Or so it seems.

# Exclusive Stakeholding

Exclusive stakeholding—in contrast to inclusive stakeholding—has created perverse outcomes during world history. Here are some ongoing current examples.

The federal deficit, private pension funds, and Social Security are examples of improper stakeholding that has evolved into instruments that plunder the funds of future stakeholders. It creates a sense of imperialism, but in the temporal rather than the spatial dimension.

Most private health insurers currently have a one-year, Tinder-type "trading" relationship with their clients. If the insurer spends dollars on a client's long-term health, such as on preventative care, the long-term economic benefits of future health savings do not accrue to the insurer. This lack of inclusive stakeholding misaligns the incentives between the insurer and the client.

Imagine if the private insurer was instead paid 5 percent of each client's cumulative health savings, relative to actuarial predictions, over ten years. This payout could be performed through a futures contract or on the blockchain through a smart contract. The insurer would thus become an investor in their clients' health, where the vested stakeholding would more effectively align incentives between the client and the insurer.

Imagine teachers being similarly rewarded—for example, with tokens of appreciation on the blockchain—for contributions their former pupils make to the world during their twenties. The amounts would be small, so that teachers would still have the incentive to teach to the whole class rather than focusing on the next "thoroughbred." This would allow teachers to be not only motivated stakeholders in bettering the future but would reward them for helping the world.

Indeed, exclusive stakeholding is a first-order cause of why large-scale systems around the world today produce perverse outcomes relative to what the system should and could produce. It's a reason why self-expanding systems start to exhibit the Byzantine reflex, the domestication, the double binds, and the race to the middle (topics covered elsewhere in the book). It's also why people around the globe are losing faith in our institutions.

It's also the first-order cause of why institutions appear to be colluding and performing ritualized behaviors rather than acting in good faith—what Dr. Eric Weinstein of Thiel Capital refers to as *Kayfabe*.[20] We make the case that what Dr. Weinstein characterizes as the contrived nature of pro wrestling is driven by the same force that selects for high-fructose corn syrup and produces cultural commodification: exclusive stakeholding.

When a network of self-expanding, self-dealing superorganisms cooperates at an even higher level as a super-superorganism—as has been enabled by the interconnectivity of seven billion people without mutual stakeholding—the sheer awe of the power asymmetry between the system and the people is enough to lead to mass surrender.

It is our contention that our best hope for finding our way out of the digestive tract of the beast is through inclusive stakeholding.

---

20. Weinstein, Eric R., "Kayfabe," Edge, October 21, 2019, https://www.edge.org/response-detail/11783.

# The Race to the Middle

Is the race to the bottom bottomless? Aren't races supposed to end?

Maybe.

If a race to the bottom becomes sufficiently egregious, a revolt by the exploited can overthrow the establishment. At least that view is often served up as a temporary salve, however fleeting, for the plague of races to the bottom everywhere.

The possibility of revolt, including those in which heads end up on the chopping block, is evident to those in power. Thus, to some extent, the oppressors have a vested interest in putting the brakes on a breakneck runaway race to the bottom, not because they have a sense of justice, but to save their own necks. Even in this situation, the power of vested self-interest is hard at work.

Concessions by those with political power—including term limits and a system of checks and balances[21]—put the brakes on the self-reinforcing, race-to-the-bottom nature of that power. For those with economic power, concessions—including progressive taxation, philanthropy, and virtue signaling[22]—put the brakes on the self-reinforcing, race-to-the-bottom nature of wealth inequality. If a revolt becomes necessary, some of the empowered may take the side of the revolutionaries, for a wide variety of stated and actual reasons.

What this means is that many a race to the bottom eventually corrects course to become a race to the middle. In some ways, the race to the middle is worse than the race to the bottom, as it deters cleansing institutions of latent extractions. On the other hand, the race to the middle has generally helped guide the trajectory of human life upwards, lifting all boats. In short, the race to the middle is a curse and a gift.

---

21. Also known as a system of checks written to the account balances of political institutions. From: Yun, Joon, Jeremy Yun, and Conrad Yun, Interdependent Capitalism: Redesigning the Social Contract through Inclusive Stakeholding [Kindle edition], February 15, 2019;
22. See https://en.wikipedia.org/wiki/Virtue_signalling.

The race to the middle is one of the tools the beast uses to maintain the status quo. It provides a salve for second-order symptoms—but not the first-order root cause—of issues, which can temporarily temper the risk of rebellion. As discussed previously, the root cause of why competition selects for power rather than efficiency is exclusionary stakeholding—or the lack of inclusive stakeholding. Once the power structures are in place, the perpetuation of hegemony through the domestication of revolutionary ardor is the beast's objective.

Here are some examples.

Many business, social, and political leaders today have cited humankind's unbelievable material progress—the number of PhD's, toilets, access to food and water, technological progress—as indicators that life is far better today than ever before. Those claims are unassailable. The associated cultural commodification, however, has produced a dispirited population that is struggling with an increasing sense of alienation, loneliness, and lack of meaning in their lives. This combination of spiritual regression and material progress lands us approximately in the local minima that is the race to the middle, where the blended average of quality of life is just good enough to deter revolt.

Other examples of the race to the middle are race and gender relations in America. Every well-intended sequential concession by the status quo has domesticated the discontent without fully addressing the underlying issues of non-inclusive stakeholding. The mixed blessing of the race to the middle can leave entire populations in no-man's land, or—in the case of the suzerainty offered to the Native Americans—in a marginally habitable habitat. Whereas the race to the bottom inspired Tecumseh to fight for justice, the race to the middle inspires casinos.

Universal basic income (UBI) is another example. It's a post-hoc salve that perpetuates a system that invariably self-generates wealth inequality—a fiat bribe of the public that distracts from fixing the underlying cause: exclusionary stakeholding. Again, treating the symptoms merely kicks the can—or the can'ts—down the road.

On the surface, universal basic income might look superficially similar to our proposal: universal basic stakeholding (UBS). In both cases, the accrual appears tethered to the success of the nation. There is, however, a small and important distinction: whereas stakeholding, as in the case of UBS, allows a direct contractual connection between the dividend and aggregate success of the nation, in the case of UBI, the connection is seen as indirect and subject to distortion.[23] Similarly, if public and private pension funds were organized around stakes rather than defined payouts, conflict between stakeholders would be reduced and alignment increased.

The race to the middle process is rapidly tranquilizing many of our institutions—with few exceptions—to the standstill of mediocrity: education, science, medicine, food, media, politics, art—you name it. It's not just, "Where have you gone Joe DiMaggio?" It's more like, "Where the hell is everybody?"

And that is the larger point. The most significant cost of the race to the middle is the opportunity cost of not setting up a race to the top of collective greatness. Whereas competition with alignment creates a race for the top, malalignment with competition surfaces power that drives the system first toward the bottom and eventually toward some equilibrium in the middle.

The race to mediocrity produces a sense of cultural blandness and banality that is not bad enough or good enough to get too excited about. Think about why the corpocracy of automobile manufacturing inevitably not only drives itself to mass produce Toyota Camrys but induces the entire industry to make approximate replicas of Camrys. It is an excellent car, but it also is stupefyingly ordinary relative to what is possible for the times. The inherent self-dealing culture of middle management, which lacks proper stakeholding at every level of the chain and are running to stand still, ensures that imagination gets winnowed out in service to a biweekly direct deposit.

---

23. This difference in perception is similar to the distinction between when an employee earns a dividend as a company stockholder versus earning a year-end bonus. In the former case, the binding nature of the dividend that comes with being a stakeholder creates a different set of motivations than a year-end performance bonus that is subject to many forces beyond appreciation of the stock's value. UBI has the potential to domesticate public resentment against self-serving institutions.

Through commodification, the race to the middle has infected almost every vector of human life, where the feckless total output of the industrial complex is the Toyota Camry of everything—tranquilizing yet tranquil, venal yet banal. A lullaby of domesticated bliss.

# Byzantine Reflex

Once an organization or an institution gains power, it has a natural incentive to protect that power and maintain the status quo.[24] In medieval times, such protection might have taken the form of a castle topped with battlements and surrounded by a moat. Modern-day institutions employ not only updated versions of a moat but use a subtler approach to protect themselves, like the one Dame Gothel used to hide Rapunzel in the Grimm fairy tale: a self-cultivated thicket.

Industrial economists understand well the tendency of powerful incumbents to use their influence on governments to construct elaborate "regulatory thickets" that inhibit competitive challenge. The phenomenon, however, is very general. In monarchical eras, courtesans constructed similarly elaborate, almost impenetrable rituals to protect their positions of influence and power. The phrase "Byzantine complexity" refers to the impossibly complicated protocols and procedures of the Byzantine Empire, which was the continuation of the Roman Empire in its eastern provinces in late antiquity and the Middle Ages.[25] The infamous rituals of the Byzantine court, however, were exceptionally complex only in comparison with the norms of the era, when most monarchs were elevated feudal lords and royal courts were relatively rough-hewn affairs.

While most of the complexity that allows modern exchange economies to exist is deeply submerged in digital protocols and, increasingly, nearly inscrutable machine learning algorithms, enough remains on the surface to make the Byzantine court look like a family affair. This is not because complexity tends to

---

24. This is also true within the "bureaucracy of the mind" that lives inside each of our brains.
25. "Guests at royal banquets were assigned titles that denoted where they could sit in relation to the emperor, whom they could talk to, and what they were allowed to discuss. Eventually, the rituals became so complex that treatises were written to help outsiders understand proper etiquette, and the emperor employed officials to teach newbies how to behave." See Palmer, Brian, "How Complicated Was the Byzantine Empire?" Slate, October 20, 2011, https://slate.com/news-and-politics/2011/10/the-byzantine-tax-code-how-complicated-was-byzantium-anyway.html.

increase within any institution over time (as was largely true of the Byzantine Empire) but because powerful incumbents have learned to use complexity as a barrier against competition.

The Byzantine Reflex refers to systems that are characterized by a tendency to self-evolve toward greater complexity and obfuscation in a way that favors the asymmetric beneficiaries of the status quo. Indeed, such systems will self-select against simplicity and transparency. A corrupt government, for example, will do nothing to stop complicating government regulations, as such obfuscation enables them to set predatory traps for the public.

Another feature of self-dealing beasts is the reduced choices offered to the people. In a rational healthcare system, for example, patients ought to be able to choose their physician and the physician ought to be able to choose the right treatment for the patient. Instead, the "beastlike" healthcare system has self-organized and consolidated its power to the point where patients often can't pick their doctors and doctors often can't choose treatments that might be best for their patients.

The larger point is this: unless interests are properly aligned through inclusive stakeholding, the natural inclinations of individuals and free markets will naturally self-assemble into the exact nightmare that libertarians fear: a bureaucracy.

This is how America, a nation built on the libertarian principles of individual freedoms (a.k.a mutually exclusive stakeholding) evolved into a restrictive legal system that constrains individual freedoms. Today, the number of laws in the nation founded on seven articles of the Constitution has been continually self-expanding to the point where the most accurate answer to the question "how many statutes are there in the United States government?" is that it is unknowable, according to the U.S. government. [26]

Here is the take-home message: without aligned interests to protect you from abuses, in any system that contains Byzantine complexity, be wary of an underlying counterparty that could be acting against your interest.

---

26. Cali, Jeanine, "Response to 'Frequent Reference Question: How Many Federal Laws Are There?'" [Library of Congress post], March 12, 2013, https://blogs.loc.gov/law/2013/03/frequent-reference-question-how-many-federal-laws-are-there/.

# On the Emergence of Language

Evolution is an "as is" phenomenon, and teleology as an explanatory style remains controversial. "Why" questions are generally shunned in science as they cannot be empirically validated with experimental tools.

With that limitation in mind, trying to explain the evolutionary emergence of human language is even more problematic, given the paucity of direct evidence. Indeed, the Linguistic Society of Paris's prohibition against debating the topic in 1866 remained influential in suppressing formal discourse on the subject in academia until very recently.[27]

Nonetheless, since the time of Darwin, people have speculated as to why language may have emerged during human evolution. Today, varying hypotheses exist as to where, when, how, and why language may have emerged, but there is scant agreement among them.[28] Furthermore, while many have attempted to link the emergence of language with the emergence of modern human behavior, there is little agreement as to the nature of this association. The full list of hypotheses about the putative link are explored elsewhere.

To that list we would like to add another potential hypothesis. What if the shift from living in kin-based social systems to living in communities of strangers—which lowers genetic alignment and increases counterparty risk—was a forcing function in the acceleration of advanced symbolic systems such as language?

When genetic alignment is higher, the need to negotiate is lower. One can assume that actions within a community are more likely to serve the interests of

---

27. Stam, J. H., Inquiries into the Origins of Language (New York: Harper and Row, 1976), 255.
28. Tallerman, M., and K. R. Gibson, The Oxford Handbook of Language Evolution (Oxford, UK: Oxford University Press, 2012).

others and the group. On the other hand, when alignment is low, interactions require a greater degree of negotiation. Subtleties and nuances matter more and the precision that comes with naming things, actions, and abstractions enhances the ability of members in a low-aligned community to negotiate more effectively.

Were these burdens a forcing function in the acceleration of human consciousness? Philosophers have long debated the role of language in our ability to experience the world. Gorgias of Leontini posited that the physical world cannot be experienced except through language. Plato and St. Augustine believed that words were merely labels applied to already existing concepts. Immanuel Kant believed language was one of many tools used by humans to experience the world.

In recent times, the theory of linguistic relativity (also known as the Sapir-Whorf hypothesis) has emerged to posit that individuals experience the world based on the language they habitually use. For example, because there was a paucity of color terminology in Homeric Greek literature, Greeks at the time are presumed not to have experienced colors as we can today.[29]

Thus, if the shift from high-alignment, kin-based social systems to low-alignment systems was a catalyst for the development of elaborate languages, then the same fundamental shift of our social evolution may also have had a hand in helping us experience the world in a far richer fashion and develop advanced thoughts.

In short, the fall from the Eden of our tribal past may have precipitated the development of human awareness, instead of the other way around. (In the standard version of the story, humans were expelled from Eden for eating an apple that led to awareness.)

A broader interpretation of the theory of linguistic relativity suggests that naming words promotes consciousness through awareness. By transitivity, those who espouse such a view could make the case that the transition of human social systems from inclusive fitness to reciprocal altruism may have been a forcing function for the emergence of human consciousness.

---

29. See https://en.wikipedia.org/wiki/Linguistic_relativity_and_the_color_naming_debate.

From an individual's life's perspective, children have no subjective memory of the time before they could name things. Fractally, from the perspective of the species, humans have no recorded memory of the time before the emergence of symbolic systems.

# On the Emergence of Math

Many precipitating factors help explain the emergence of advanced symbolic systems during human evolution. We posit that the fundamental shift of human communities—from one predominantly based on kin altruism to one predominantly based on reciprocal altruism—has played a role in the development of advanced symbolic systems.

During the kin tribe era, we could generally trust that others would act with our best interests at heart without doing an undue amount of due diligence. Today, reciprocal altruism is the dominant form of human transaction, and we now have to count the beans to ascertain if the transactions are fair. Consuming the counterparty risk of strangers is a far cry from suckling the milk of a mother who loved us unconditionally.

Advanced symbolic systems no doubt increase the evolutionary fitness of social systems based on kin altruism. These systems, however, are even more important for social systems that have to rely predominantly on reciprocal altruism. Counterparty risk is far higher among genetic strangers than genetic relatives. Things and concepts have to be more precisely defined and accounted for when negotiating with counterparties who are incentivized to exploit rather than serve each other.

A specific example of this hypothesis as it applies to advanced symbolic systems is worth further discussion: the emergence of modern numerical systems based on linear scales. In highly aligned social systems, where the conveyance of numerical information is on behalf of a relative rather than against a stranger, representation of quantities can be expressed on a compressive scale where there is high resolution at low numbers and low resolution at high numbers.[30] For instance, as a default, a language might only need to contain the symbols for one, two, several, many, and innumerable.

The benefits of using compressive scales to express quantities are the following. They efficiently represent a wide dynamic range of quantities—the way a Richter Scale is efficient. Second, compressive scales represent quantities according to relevance. When something is scarce, such as bananas in wintertime, being able to discriminate between the quantities one and two matters. On the other hand, there is no fitness relevance to being able to distinguish between a high number of bananas, such as 280 and 281. Third, ecological features such as distance to a predator or prey present themselves to our sensory systems on compressive scales. Imagine a line of trees in a forest; trees closer to us appear farther apart from each other than trees that are far from us, and those closer to us will impact our fitness more than those farther away. Finally, everything in nature occurs through recursion of underlying "rules of nature." As such, everything natural is compounding, a phenomenon better expressed on compressive scales than on linear scales.

Linear scales (equidistance between every consecutive number), however, serve a transactional world better than compressive scales. From the perspective of a counterparty transaction, high resolution at high numbers matters even more than at lower numbers. For example, spending $25,000 for a car versus $24,000 is a huge discrepancy for a customer with a net worth of $30,000; therefore, it is vital that the consumer "senses" the $1,000 difference. A linear scale enables them to sense this far better than a compressive scale.

It is intuitively appealing to speculate that the emergence of linear notational systems for numbers in the modern world in multiple cultures, including India, Assyria, Sumer, Rome, and China, was a function of the rising counterparty risk in transactions associated with the transition from a high-alignment world to a

---

30. See Yun, Joon, Compound Thinking (Kindle edition), 2015, https://www.amazon.com/Compound-Thinking-Joon-Yun-ebook/dp/B015GCMHFC/ref=sr_1_1?ie=UTF8&qid=1547931605&sr=8-1&keywords=compound+thinking+joon+yun.

low-alignment world. More specifically, the development of linear scales catalyzed trade among counterparties (reciprocal altruism).

Indeed, the oldest known human counting systems—the small clay tokens invented in the Zagros region of Iran around 4000 BCE,[31] the pictographs on tablets representing numerals in 3500 BCE,[32] and the abstract numerals dissociated from the thing being counted in 3100 BCE[33]—are thought to have been developed to facilitate trade of commodities.[34] Sumerians invented arithmetic soon thereafter, including addition, subtraction, multiplication, and division, to manage their grain trade.[35] Thereafter, more and more advanced mathematics began to emerge as trade flourished.[36]

There is no doubt that linear mathematics has proven its worth. High resolution at high numbers is the only way to create the kind of precision at high numbers that would allow us to land a rocket on the faraway moon. On the other hand, the near complete hegemony of linear-scale mathematics over compressive-scale mathematics also comes with a significant social cost. All natural phenomena occur through the recursion of underlying fundamentals, resulting in compounding outcomes. Linear-scale mathematics does a poor job of capturing and studying compounding phenomena, which happen everywhere in the natural world.

Notice that everything in nature curves and that all the straight lines you see are man-made.

Humans relying on linear-scale mathematics tend to significantly underestimate the compounding effects of both growth and decline, which would be gauged far more effectively on compressive scales. Black swans tend to get underpriced as a result.

---

31. See Schmandt-Besserat, Denise, "Two Precursors Of Writing: Plain and Complex Tokens," December 8, 2008, http://en.finaly.org/index.php/Two_precursors_of_writing:_plain_and_complex_tokens.
32. Schmandt-Besserat, Denise, How Writing Came About (Austin: University of Texas Press, 1996).
33. Schmandt-Besserat, How Writing Came About.
34. See https://en.wikipedia.org/wiki/History_of_ancient_numeral_systems.
35. Nissen, H. J., P. Damerow, and R. Englund, Archaic Bookkeeping (Chicago: University of Chicago Press, 1993).
36. See, for example, https://en.wikipedia.org/wiki/Topology.

# Memetic Parallax

What comes immediately after "world peace"? Civil war.

Humans tend to form groups that disagree with each other, just as a single cell must divide through the process of mitosis to enable the growth of an organism. Polarization isn't a bug of human social software. It's a feature.

From a multilevel selection perspective, evolution selects for systems with features that increase evolutionary capacity: imperfect replication, sexual reproduction, predation, programmed death, memetics, etc.[37] Add to this list memetic parallax, which is the tendency of meme groups to diverge into competing views.[38]

The tendency toward groupthink driven by memetic algorithms can trap systems in local minima in the adaptive landscape that impede evolutionary novelty and constrain fitness. From a multilevel selection perspective, a certain degree of trait diversity (meme or physical) and conflict within a system promotes that system's robustness and evolutionary capacity. The propensity to disagree with others—many incentives and disincentives influence the process—can promote overall system fitness.

Indeed, at a macro level, the theory of evolutionary capacity predicts that selection favors systems that generate feature parallax (diversity over consensus), especially when it promotes conflict to a degree that optimizes competition and accelerates evolution.

For example, predator-prey competition can be viewed as a feature parallax that increases evolutionary capacity for both parties. In cultural evolution, the

37. Wilson, D. S., Does Altruism Exist? Culture, Genes, and the Welfare of Others (New Haven, CT: Yale University Press, 2015).
38. Socratic dialogues and Hegelian dialectic both reflect the fundamental role of memetic parallax in human inquiry. See Hegel, G. W. F., The Phenomenology of Spirit (Oxford, UK: Oxford University Press, 2018).

fragmentation of socio-political-economic philosophies such as socialism and capitalism represent ideological parallax that benefits the overall system.

Sexual reproduction is another system that promotes genotype and phenotype parallax (male vs. female). The parallax is associated with collaboration as well as competition between the sexes and intrasexual competition. The competing agendas promote vast increases in novel features, including cognition and social behaviors. Sexual reproduction is an example of active, positive selection for traits among gender counterparts with highly aligned interest in a joint venture (i.e., offspring) in which each owns a 50 percent vested interest (or less for males, given paternal uncertainty).[39]

When there is trust, respect, and alignment (genetic and otherwise) between individuals or groups, the parallax can be highly beneficial to the individuals and to the combined superorganism. A second opinion from a trusted partner is a significant value-add in partnerships, teams, and marriages. Without trust and respect, memetic parallax can lead to dysfunctional polarization, including war.

A fundamental feature of diversity is often overlooked. With common ground (inclusive stakeholding), diversity can be mutually beneficial. On the other hand, diversity without common ground (exclusive stakeholding) can lead to separatism.

When aggressive Balkanization occurs, individuals and groups also tend to unify internally, to merge, form meme alliances, and cooperate—again, many incentives and disincentives influence the process—to compete against outside groups. When facing a common external enemy, we tend to settle our internal disputes and unite against the enemy until a larger consensus (peace) results.[40]

Once the enemy is dissipated, memetic parallax reemerges. The victors of WWII entered peace discussions with a spirit of international cooperation and exited with divergent agendas. There's wisdom to the notion that a war defend-

---

39. The standard explanation for why sexual reproduction evolved was increased diversity. We propose a more salient reason: that vested interest in our offspring is a powerful driver of the careful and motivated selection of our reproductive partner's traits.

40. The rise of nationalism following the unification of warring factions in Japan instigated imperialism—a pattern repeated often around the world when clans settle their differences in favor of common aims. Imperialism and colonialism are outlets that feed the beast and keep internal harmony between warring tribes.

ing humanity against a common enemy such as an alien invasion would diffuse existing ideological stalemates, at least until the victory parade.

When a group Balkanizes into many groups, an important second trait of social systems deters further fragmentation—the hive mentality. From a total-system evolutionary-capacity perspective, there is a tradeoff: parallax is preferred over consensus, but continued parallax and over-fragmentation are also costly. "Us versus them" campaigns require retaining and growing the "us." Social systems are wired to consolidate and grow their membership and their power as superorganisms. That said, under certain conditions, meme groups can atomize considerably to the point of information anarchy, as has happened in the case of dietary recommendations.

Selection favors dynamic systems capable of both consensus memetics and memetic parallax in a context-dependent fashion. A fractal is apparent. Evolution favors systems with capacity for two features that are themselves in competitive parallax: the tendency for groupthink and the tendency for parallax.

Thus, the arcs of human and evolutionary histories are poised to teeter between competition and cooperation in a never-ending vacillation across the different scales of biology and time. Peace will follow war, and war will follow peace. And so on.

That is, parallax can also occur along the temporal axis, rather than only at any one moment in time. The Hegelian dialectic—and to some extent the entire intellectual history of Marxism—is built on this. Dualities that evolve over time— the cyclical procession of thesis, antithesis, and synthesis—delineate the progress of human society. Now, of course, the absurdity of Hegel was his announcement that the early nineteenth century was the termination of this historical procession of thesis, antithesis, and synthesis.

Others, too, have tried to make similar claims. Francis Fukuyama wrote in *The End of History and the Last Man* (1992) that the neoclassical liberal state was the end of history. All of that is juxtaposed against the capitalist model, where progress is the persistent story of heroic individuals overcoming adversaries. But neither Marxism nor capitalism can lay total claim to the progress of humanity.

But it doesn't really matter if this is the end of history, if this is the final synthesis, or if this is just the next stage. The point is that Inclusive Stakeholding is the imminent next thing that stands in stark contrast with exclusive stakeholding of history—as an intertemporal memetic parallax.

# Mob Mentality in the Technology Age

In her treatise on the psychology of moral panics, Dr. Maia Newley explores the innate vulnerability of human communities to mass hysteria: even well-educated and apparently rational intellectuals (Hobbes, Bacon, Milton, Locke) were not immune to joining the broad public in becoming convinced that evil witches with great powers were imperiling England.[41]

Such mass hysteria can occur at any scale of social aggregation. For example, Ekbom's syndrome is a delusional disorder in which individuals incorrectly believe they are infested with parasites and they often compulsively gather "evidence" to present to others. Pairs of people also can famously exhibit mob mentality.[42] For example, *folie à deux* is when two people, typically a patient and a spouse, share such a delusion, cultivating an "us versus them" attitude, which can lead to magnificent triumphs or to Bonnie-and-Clyde-like calamities. In *folie à plusieurs*, large groups share a delusion and selectively aggregate the "evidence" that supports their collective belief. Witch hunts fall into this category.[43]

So, are witch hunts a thing of the past? Hardly. Groupthink—including its most extreme form, mob mentality—is an evolutionarily selected feature of

---

41. See https://www.researchgate.net/publication/276997801_THE_JACOBEAN_WITCH_CRAZE_-_THE_CASE_FOR_FOLIES_A_PLUSIEURS_Psychopathology_of_Early_Modern_Folk_Devils_and_Moral_Panics.
42. Being madly in love can be seen as an example of a shared delusion.
43. See https://www.researchgate.net/publication/276997801_THE_JACOBEAN_WITCH_CRAZE_-_THE_CASE_FOR_FOLIES_A_PLUSIEURS_Psychopathology_of_Early_Modern_Folk_Devils_and_Moral_Panics,

living systems that is not going away anytime soon. Moreover, as a consequence of the increasing interconnectedness through technology, we are more than ever vulnerable to mob behavior.

First, let's discuss mobbing as a feature. For most of human history, kin skin in the game shared across individuals has enabled us humans to coordinate our collective behaviors as a "superorganism" that transcends individual boundaries. What is true of genetic affinity also turns out to be true of memetic affinity. Genetic affinity creates the motivation—inclusive fitness—for individuals to coordinate behaviors as a group superorganism; similarly, memetic affiliation creates the common language that allows groups to function as groups, rather than as collections of individuals.

In this way, groupthink is an evolutionary win for both the individual and the superorganism. Rearing offspring, shared defense, resource acquisition, migration, and communication all work better in a kin-based group. In prehistoric times we would call memetic affiliation "tribal beliefs"; today, memetic affiliation might be referred to as corporate culture or patriotism—many non-familial groups appropriate the term "family" to foster cohesiveness. It's the instinct that makes parents of children on sports teams believe that the referee's calls are made against their own team unfairly. The root is the same: our power to communicate, coordinate, and learn—the essence of our evolutionary advantage as a social species. Without groupthink, we—all of us—quite simply would not exist. For the foregoing reasons, groupthink is clearly a feature of human evolution.

As technology increases information liquidity, the role of memetic algorithms in coordinating human group behaviors through all of these categories is rising. On one hand, this is good news. New types of useful communities are made possible by virtue of the vast amount of technology-enabled connectivity now available.

The problem comes when mobbing tendencies get misappropriated and become liabilities in our dizzyingly global and interconnected world, which has taken us away from kin tribes. Evolutionary dislocation can render our propensity for groupthink into a bug, especially when memetic algorithms reflect external interests rather than the interest of those in the group. Collective consciousness can easily be subverted into becoming a memetic mob that is under the spell of companies, political groups, foreign nations, social movements, etc.. Systemic fear is the most common trigger for individuals to surrender their personal agency in service of groupthink, and examples abound. Consider the rising degree of confirmation bias and polarization between political groups in the United States from 2016 to the present.

Here is the big picture. Previously, decentralized bioalgorithms distributed across individuals performed coordinated functions, such as "falling in love" or kin skin in the game, in service of superorganisms. That is, mobbing occurs when decentralized memetic algorithms distributed across individuals perform coordinated functions in service of the superorganism. What has changed in the technology age is that mobbing can be hijacked by other superorganisms to serve external interests. Today, memetic superorganisms everywhere are competing with each other to hijack the bioalgorithms of individuals to perform functions that serve external interests.

Inclusive stakeholding may be our best chance to deter continued self-serving misappropriations of collective consciousness.

# Neutron Bomb of
# Human Sociality

On February 1, 1950, the USSR government sent a letter[44] to the U.S. Secretary of State sharing the findings of the 1949 Khabarovsk War Crime Trials held between 25-31 December 1949.[45] In 1950, the USSR also published in English a large volume of official documents related to the trial including verbatim testimonies and documentary evidence that conflicted with America's account of Japan's role in World War II.[46] [47] In the context of the Cold War and growing distrust of the USSR, the United States dismissed the trial and its findings as communist propaganda until the 1980s, near the end of the Cold War.[48] The book containing verbatim testimonies and documentary evidence published by the USSR has long been out of print, but it recently surfaced on Google Books in 2015.[49] The West's dismissal of the Khabarovsk trial illustrates the influence that ideology has on our ability to make fair cross-ideology assessments.[50]

This case is an example of distrust bias: the tendency to discount *specific* evidence or ideas—even potentially beneficial ones—if the source is otherwise *generally* considered untrustworthy. Distrust bias is a companion concept to hostile attribution bias, which is the paranoid tendency to interpret benign actions as hostile when the source of the action is considered untrustworthy.[51] Humans are

44. Page 51 of https://www.archives.gov/files/iwg/japanese-war-crimes/select-documents.pdf
45. https://en.wikipedia.org/wiki/Khabarovsk_War_Crime_Trials
46. https://en.wikipedia.org/wiki/Khabarovsk_War_Crime_Trials
47. https://books.google.com/books?id=ARojAAAAMAAJ&printsec=frontcover#v=onepage&q&f=false
48. https://link.springer.com/article/10.1007/BF02448905
49. https://play.google.com/books/reader?id=ARojAAAAMAAJ&hl=en&pg=GBS.PA10
50. https://link.springer.com/article/10.1007/BF02448905
51. Nasby, W., Hayden, B., & DePaulo, B. M. (1980). Attributional bias among aggressive boys to interpret

prone to distrust bias not only at the interpersonal level—we've all seen scorned lovers discredit every action of their ex—but also at ideological or national levels.

As is the case with hostile attribution bias, distrust bias tends to form feed-forward loops: interpretation of actions as untrustworthy increases the sense of distrust. This is when memetic parallax turns into its malignant, polarizing variant.

Today, America is mired in a Civil Cold War that foments political polarization, gender wars, class warfare, ageism, sectionalism, etc. Around the world, similar ideological Cold Wars are on the rise everywhere, not only along nationalistic and ethnic lines, but along virtually every line of human identity.

It should be noted that the physical brain trauma caused by an external force often induces a secondary trauma called coup-contrecoup injury: the traumatic force in one direction provokes a traumatic force in the other direction. When it comes to the memetic trauma caused to the brain by an external force, the same coup-contracoup insult can also happen. For example, the rise of political extremism on one side induces political extremism on the other side through a series of mutually escalating reprisals. Similarly, misogyny begets misandry, which begets misogyny in the gender wars of today.

The social algorithm of memetic mobs works this way: anyone who attempts to point out the merits of an idea that has been developed or espoused by an ideological opponent are branded as "sympathizers." Such shaming is a behavioral feature of mobs, empowering the memetic superorganism to silence dissident memes and assert control over individual free expression.

The consequences of distrust bias driving ideological polarization in the age of technology could be enormous and potentially disastrous. Once the common ground has been poisoned, the instinct to take the opposite position is innate and blinding, not unlike how some teenagers—who are biologically wired to leave the nest at the onset of puberty but are kept in the nest longer given modern social structures—rebel by doing the exact opposite of what the parents ask of them, regardless of the merits of the ask. More broadly, the tendency is for an ideolog-

unambiguous social stimuli as displays of hostility. Journal of Abnormal Psychology, 89(3), 459.

ical group to adopt a position opposite their ideological enemy, regardless of the position's merit, under the assumption that whatever position the latter adopts must be a bad idea and opposed. Anyone falling short of opposing every position of the enemy will be named a sympathizer and outcast from the in-group by the ideological mob.

The resulting oppositionalism is self-escalating. The attack by memetic superorganism A towards memetic superorganism B triggers a fear response in the target memetic superorganism, which increases its power to control internal individualism through mobbing—as seen during the McCarthy era and today. This allows the memetic superorganism B to sharpen its weapons and counterattack against the attacking memetic superorganism A, triggering the fear in superorganism A, which allows greater control over its group through mobbing. This cycle is mutually reinforcing, promoting polarization.

The heightened mutual suspicion can spill over into other domains, not unlike a nuclear chain reaction: the radioactive energy of one topic is the input that triggers the nucleus of another topic to split into two, setting off a cascade. What results is a mutation that turns human sociality into a cancer.

Who would want this to happen?

For extractive capitalists such as click-bait media companies or commerically motivated political fundraising machines that profit from polarization, the resulting social pollution is merely an externality—not unlike the environmental pollution of industrialists. It's not something they want to see happen, and willful blindness helps them in that regard.

Foreign governments that *do* want to see this happen—whose aim is to undermine another nation—play the game at a higher level. They can foment memetic fragmentation and internal combustion of another nation merely by paying to subvert the same profiteering instinct of click-bait media companies and commerically motivated political fundraising machines—or any mercenary social, political, and economic institution.

In essence, all it takes to take down civilization is natural inclinations, free-markets, and exclusive stakeholding—one company not having a properly aligned stake in the nation's success, one nation not having a properly aligned stake in another nation's success, etc.

In a narrow sense, the fear of potential mutual nuclear annihilation during the Cold War was subverted by institutions to domesticate individuality. In a broader sense, exclusive stakeholding is the invisible neutron bomb of human sociality that has already detonated; it is manifesting as a growing cancer globally—the extractive behaviors of humanity. Meanwhile, inclusive stakeholding is our best chance for a cure.

In his novel *One Flew Over the Cuckoo's Nest*, Ken Kesey explores the power that institutions wield over individuals through subversion of innate human instincts in the Cold War era. That power is nested in Nurse Ratched who holds dominion over her patients in the psychiatric hospital. She manifests that power in part through leveraging the self-dealing instincts of inmates: she baits them to disclose damaging information about each other in exchange for her granting favorable wake-up times.

She herself is a tool, an agent of a larger authoritarian system that maintains authority by undermining it subjects' ability to revolt against the system. In that sense, even the Cold War itself is an example of two superorganisms—America and USSR—who have been domesticated by an even larger system-wide superorganism that keeps each nation (1) fighting against each other and (2) domesticating their own people by pitting individuals against each other.

A fractal recursion is evident: a global superorganism domesticating Cold War superpowers by inducing them to fight; each Cold War superpower domesticating its satellite states by inducing them to internally fight; each state domesticating its citizens by inducing them to infight; a veterans mental hospital domesticating war victims by inducing them to infight. In essence, the new global superorganism encoded through exclusive stakeholding destroys the prior superorganisms by atomizing them into their individual components.[52]

---

52. The self-expanding beast does the same thing to science, atomizing systemic concepts into it's inscrutable individual components.

The central irony is that Kesey depicts the system, not the inmates, as "cuckoo." In using subversion to undermine Nurse Ratched's subversion, McMurphy turns the cuckoo's game on its head. In nature, the cuckoo preys on other birds' nests, but in Kesey's novel it's the free-wheeling geese that fly over the cuckoo's own nest. The narrative is part of Kesey's own revolt against what he sees as the broader tyranny of American institutions in the 1950s: tranquilization marketed as tranquility and domestication marketed as domestic bliss. Yet if you wind the cuckoo clock five dozen years forward, we've circled back to where we were. Institutions everywhere are competing to control individual minds, witch hunts are polarizing the nation, and modern day "Merry Pranksters" are running to the hills with psychedelics.

It's crazy.

# Duality Is the Reality

So how do we turn the tide on the epidemic of selfish behaviors that have corroded our institutions and eroded our communities? We believe the first step is to bust the central myth of the past few millennia: that there is a separation between good and evil people in the world.

In the real world, individuals are not *either* good *or* evil. We are all *both* good *and* evil. There are no groups of heroes versus groups of beasts. There are no groups of white knights versus groups of black nights. There are polarities everywhere, but also shades of grey. Everyone harbors both the Yin and the Yang. This duality is a truth that's neither palatable to the ego nor marketable for those who want to sell a story.

Yet, this duality is the reality.

At the end of the day, everyone participates in the greater system in a way that causes some harm to others, however subtle or remote, but there is a general blindness to this reality. Our minds tend to downplay our role in the harm we cause others and overplay the role of others in the harm we experience.

In the preceding essays, we mentioned that self-expanding, race-to-the-bottom beasts are everywhere—in the food we eat, the social networks we track, the pills we take, the sports teams we follow, the political machines we support, and the self-help groups we join. What we miss—nearly all of us, nearly all of the time—is something more fundamental: that all of these self-dealing, race-to-the-bottom organizations have grown out of the same global petri-dish of misaligned incentives that is modernity. And all of them feed on the same set of primal instincts that allowed us humans to survive prehistory.

What's notable is that we have little trouble seeing the evil in others. We easily recognize it and call it out in the institutions of which we are not a part. Corporate executives and entrepreneurs have no difficulty recognizing the self-dealing beast that is government bureaucracy; noble civil servants (a.k.a. government bureaucrats) have similarly little difficulty recognizing the self-dealing beasts on Wall Street and in Silicon Valley. Pulitzer Prize-winning news organizations understand that their duty is to reveal the self-dealing beast that is the political system. Politicians assert that it is their duty to reveal the fundamental corruption of the media.

The general blindness to this reality is evidenced by Godwin's Law, the Internet rule asserting that, "as an online discussion grows longer, the probability of a comparison involving Nazis or Hitler approaches 1." Importantly, this law holds, regardless of the characteristics or the views of the individuals engaged in such discussions. It evidences the fact that our society has evolved (or cultivated) a deep-seated need to experience not only as evil but as absolute evil all who oppose our many and varied heroic quests.

We all gaze across the moats that divide us and point to the self-dealing beasts on the other side. We Occupy. We Tea Party. We Yellow Jacket. We sue. We counter-sue and counter-counter-sue. We Tweet, we post. Above all, we attack. We do so fueled by the conviction that the wind of history is behind us.

Yet, even if we were to prevail in demolishing all the beasts we perceive around us, others who want to take us down would see us as the beast.

And so, we proceed on seven billion Hero's Journeys that add up to a single collective ride on the Carousel of History.

———————

The following story offers a further illustration of how hard it is to detect our role in the suffering of others.

We have a labradoodle puppy. He is descended from a lineage of canines that hunted and killed for their meals. He harbors a dog-eat-dog past—we all do—but lives in a dog-eat-dog-food present. He's been bred and domesticated to be friendly, furry, pettable, and even hypoallergenic for my allergy-prone dad; he definitely has not been bred for his ability to hunt. He couldn't hurt most creatures if he tried. If he started eating what he killed, we'd probably give him away. His benign nature is the reason we didn't keep the receipt when we brought him home.

That's not to say that the killing has stopped. He is eating dog food made from living creatures that were killed out of sight by "the machine." "The machine" is probably one of those self-expanding beasts that profit from a system that we feed with our purchases. What about humans? Are we dog-eat-dog people, or are we good, innocent people who bask in the illusion of domesticated bliss while displacing the "evil" onto a system that we disparage but nonetheless feed into (and thus are a part of)?

By and large, we have chosen the latter narrative. Rather than accepting our total identity—that each of us is simultaneously the beast and the hero, the good and the evil, the problem and the solution—we have chosen, through memetic parallax, to segregate these identities. We have chosen to believe in the myth of separatism.

In separatism, we identify ourselves as the good people. We identify the opposing side as inherently bad people. If we think the other team is the good team, we switch sides. To that bad team we assign the role of monsters, beasts, legendary creatures, and the devil, all the while being blind to the possibility that we too might have a beastly side. We are blind to the fact that the other side sees us as the monsters.

We are both good and evil but find it difficult to accept that duality.

---

In many ways, our sociality has been devolving from where we started. Over time, we have abandoned the reality of duality in favor of separatism. Our worsening blindness stems in no small part from the myths we hold on to.

In the story of Eden, there's a serpent with no prior allegorical ontogenesis (more on this character later) who seduces Eve, who then seduces Adam. Adam and Eve then consume a forbidden apple from the Tree of Knowledge. Our first ancestors' disobedience and expulsion from Eden led to our awareness of the separateness of good and evil.

An outcome of separatism is the construction and expansion of the concept of self, the ego. This speaks to the possibility that the self movement has been going on for a long time.

Maybe time was timeless in the Eden of kin tribes. Maybe leaving the hearth of our kin tribe marked the beginning of time as we know it. As the kin tribe connections slowly disintegrated and our sociality devolved, instead of time *being* current, it started moving upstream *against* the current—the journey to a savage inward darkness. More and more, we acted against, instead of for, the interests of others.

Within a nuclear family, the human experience is characterized by unconditional love, service, and sacrifice. For nearly everyone in the nuclear family, these behaviors are programmed and promoted by the 50 percent genetic vested interest they have in each other.

Over the generations, however, the shared genetic vested interest gets diluted more quickly than you might realize. Grandchildren have 0.25 of their genes in common, great-grandchildren only 0.125. After ten generations, the degree of genetic correlation among descendants is as low as 0.0009. In other words, they are genetic strangers.[53] Assuming twenty years between generations, the original nuclear family spawns a network of strangers in a short two hundred years.

Among strangers who lack kin skin in the game, self-dealing instincts mathematically overwhelm kin altruistic instincts. Some collaborative behaviors among strangers (e.g., the reciprocal altruism or conditional love among friends) can create bonds. It is the extractive, nefarious, and even predatory behaviors among strangers, however, that cast a shadow over the human experience.

Where that breakpoint occurs is a matter of circumstance. On the one hand, there's fratricide, when the downstream stakes motivate that behavior. On the other hand, there's philanthropy for genetic strangers on other continents. The most important point here is that, starting from the original house, vested interest *between* nuclear families declines over the generations, even as the vested interest *within* nuclear families stays intact.

---

53. Different cultures have different standards as to what the border is between stranger and relative.

From the point of view of any one person, the contrast between altruistic behaviors among kin groups and transactional behaviors among strangers is readily apparent. We all start with the original experience of our mother's unconditional love in utero, and later experience the extractive behavior of strangers. We first become aware of light when we exit the tunnel of unconditional love. From that moment forward we become increasingly aware of duality.

That moment is worth a good cry.

———————————

To some extent, the stress of dealing with strangers is diffused by forces of mutual repulsion. Diaspora is typically couched in a lovely story of families adventuring forward, but it's not unequally motivated by the dispersion instinct propelled by the stress of dealing with low-aligned relatives. Take one's nuclear family and hit the road.

The broader point is that people become aware of good behaviors and bad behaviors. It is at this point that we slip into a fallacy.

We tend to group behaviors into two disparate clusters and build simplistic, black-and-white archetypes. It is as if one thing embodies all the evil and the other thing embodies all the good. Once these archetypes have been sculpted, creating stories is fairly trivial. Think of all the stories we've told ourselves and each other about monsters, legendary creatures, hobbits, trolls, devils, angels, heroes, and gods. It's not only trivial…it's unstoppable.

We, of course, tend to think of ourselves as the heroes fighting against the bad guys. If we pay closer attention to reality, we observe something different. The most evil self-dealing Wall Street crook did it for the unconditional love of his kids. The most evil self-dealing monarch did it to give the kingdom to his beloved kids. As we self-righteously judge the evil behaviors of strangers while showing unconditional love for our own children, we are blind to the fact that we *are* the self-dealing stranger that others judge.

The disdain is mutual. So is the self-flattery. We can see each other's hypocrisies but be blind to our own.

In reality, we are all mixed parts of good and bad, yet something made us see the world in black and white, made us believe that there are separate heroes and monsters. And something made us believe that we are the heroes. What made us believe that?

It was the stories we've told ourselves.

———————————

Was duality—that notion each person embodies both good and evil—the "original" story that was displaced by the modern myth of separatism?

At the beginning of this book, we praised parental love. Then we chafed at the nepotism it spawned. We then lauded competition for shaping prosperity. Then we impugned it for creating a world in which we gorge on high-fructose corn syrup and the Kardashians. You can feel the tension of these self-contradictions. In one minute, an institution is our story's hero. In the next, it is the beast we are attacking. The distinction between hero and beast comes across indistinctly at best.

No concept embodies the tension inherent in this duality better than the Chinese *taijitu* symbol of yin and yang. Yin and yang beautifully express both symmetry and opposition. The mutuality of yin and yang is dynamic, with each force begetting the other in a never-ending cycle. According to the philosophy represented by the yin and yang symbol, all aspects of existence flow from this cycle of opposing forces, including flow itself.

Independence and interdependence are the yin and yang of human coexistence. Neither extreme can stake a claim as the optimum modality for human sociality.

Based on yin and yang, we should be at the forefront of the rise of *contrecoup* forces—a swing back to tribalism as a rejection of the hug of globalization—an embrace that is increasingly being given with knives held behind backs.

The countercultural swing back to tribalism would restore balance. But does that mean it's a good thing? If it's meant to be a good thing, it sure doesn't feel that way. Today, deep fractures seem to appear daily along every tribal element of human identity: gender, race, geography, wealth, age, and politics. The tragedy is that these tribal hurrahs might prove as phony as the much-maligned product SPAM when it first appeared as a poor replacement for meat, and later (when referring to junk email) as an even worse replacement for a friend's handwritten letter. If loyalty is a fleeting and tradable commodity, is it still loyalty? Without the kin skin in the game that existed in our original homes, true loyalty will remain as elusive within the hastily gathered "tribes" variously encamped in today's divided world as it has been since the beginning of the human diaspora tens of thousands of years ago. Rather than healing the wounds of alienation, today's tribalism throws salt in them.

That's hardly the type of future anyone would dream of—whether or not it accomplishes karmic rebalancing. Yet, that everyone-for-themselves nightmare is exactly what looms as the sun sets on this brief and remarkable interlude known as human history—a continuation of the rat race that devolves into a frenzied effort to assume the fetal position.

So where is this damn transformation we were promised? Where is the apotheosis? Haven't we gone on enough pilgrimages, attended enough Burning Mans, and disturbed enough natives about their strange brews[54] to find whatever it is we were seeking? How is it that, every time we set our compass for home, we find ourselves back in the wilderness? Seven billion people in the backseat want to know: "Are we there yet?"

We are all just a little bit tired.

Can't we just 3D print the Holy Grail?

---

In case that allusion isn't familiar to you, the Holy Grail is a legendary motif from the myths that originated in the era of courtly love. The relic was first described by Chrétien de Troyes around 1190 in *Perceval, le Conte du Graal,* a romantic story famous for being unfinished—as all stories about unrequited love ought to be. The term "holy grail" has since become synonymous with an unattainable goal that is sought for its great significance.

54. See https://en.wikipedia.org/wiki/Ayahuasca.

So, is our chase for the Great Society a fool's journey? Should the chase remain an unattained quest? Is the aspiration alone good enough?

Maybe.

If we, the authors, thought so, we wouldn't have bothered putting fingertips to keys. We started you on this particular journey because we believe the idea of a Great Society is not only possible but *probable* and *imminent*.

Why? Because the answers are right in front of us.

We're at that "tap your heels together three times" moment when we realize that we have had the power to change our story all along.

The answers are hiding in every great myth and every enduring story. They are hiding in every email we send, in every glance at another human, and in every detail of our everyday lives. They are hiding in worn world history textbooks and in today's endless array of dystopian headlines. If we only were to look.

That's because, seen through a wider lens, the arc of human experience as we know it has been nothing more than an epiphenomenon of our search for something new to replace the inclusive fitness of the tribal era as the rhythm of our shared existence. That's eminently doable.

The elusive chalice not only has been hiding in plain sight—we've been drinking from it.

––––––––––––––

Dominoes of history like the Fall of Man and the Fall of Rome are still falling today. We haven't reached, or created, that inflection point of history where we finally bring the inclusive ethos of the kin village to the global village. That inflection point—to which we would assign the year zero—remains on the far horizon. Thus, we have before us an opportunity, and an obligation, of epic proportions.

# Revolutionary Thinking

Before the time of written words, oral stories were like people: older versions died, and evolved versions that suited the changing contexts emerged.

All that changed with the invention of writing.

Written stories could outlive their storytellers and compete with descendants' stories. The Gutenberg press accelerated the replication of written stories and enabled the masses to access a growing diversity of stories and formulate their own views.

It was in this setting that a particular book collector in Kraków used the power of books to challenge one of the great ancient stories: that we (planet earth) are the center of the universe. Nicolaus Copernicus amassed a sizable library of astronomy books during the late fifteenth century, and in 1549 he published *On the Revolutions of Heavenly Spheres,* his own synthesis of the newly unleashed information. In his book, Copernicus transformed a convoluted, geocentric model of planetary motion into the elegant heliocentric model that we have today. All prior stories had us as the center of existence, thus the notion that our lives were orbiting around a body other than our own planet was nothing short of earth shattering.

Indeed, the conceptual reframing of existing, seemingly esoteric data to explain the revolution of celestial bodies was so radical that the word "revolution" became synonymous with the now-familiar notion of overthrowing an established system. Dominoes have been falling ever since…think the American Revolution, French Revolution, the Internet Revolution, the Blockchain Revolution, and the Artificial Intelligence Revolution.

Today, we are a quarter century into the Internet Revolution. As profound as the impact of Gutenberg's printing press was on the spread of ideas that helped spark the Euro-centric Renaissance, it pales in comparison to the liberation of knowledge achieved through the Internet. This begs the following question: who will be the Copernicus of our time? Our da Vinci? Our Michaelangelo?

On the one hand, looking to the Copernican Revolution for inspiration may feel like a stale analogy that we've moved far beyond; our understanding of astronomy and physics is—with due apology—light years ahead of where we were in the middle of the last millennium.

On the other hand, the Copernican Revolution might just be the perfect analogy for the revolution of our social contract with each other. The social version of the Copernican Revolution could do to egocentrism what the astronomical version did to its anagramic cousin, geocentrism: make someone else the central star of our lives.

# The Ouroboros

Past efforts suggest that trying to get people to understand that we might not be the center of the universe is non-trivial. Self-centrism has an innate appeal that other-centrism can only envy. The battle between them is akin to Goliath versus David, but without a slingshot.

Those who have put their skin in the game to try to get people to accept the idea of putting others at the center of life have paid a large price. Jesus gave up his life. Copernicus feared the potential reaction to his book, and his own reaction upon being presented the first printing was to drop dead.[55] Galileo Galilei, found guilty of heresy for carrying on the Copernican view, was sentenced to indefinite confinement and forced to read seven penitential psalms a week. In the spirit of kin skin in the game, his daughter Maria Celeste relieved him of that punishment by securing ecclesiastical permission to take it upon herself.[56]

When defending an underdog position in a memetic parallax, Galileo's fate exemplifies the perils of resistance against self-dealing, self-expanding beasts. The years leading up to his trial were characterized by the typical escalation of mob mentality, unnecessary theater, and polarization of camps. If anything, opposition to heliocentrism became entrenched. It wasn't until after Isaac Newton published *Principia* in 1687—nearly half a century after Galileo's death—that the heliocentric view became generally accepted.[57]

Is there another way for an underdog to win without throwing stones, fighting through the resistance, and alienating—or being alienated by—the very opponent they are trying to persuade?

55. Bell, E. T., The Development of Mathematics (New York: Dover, 1992/1940).
56. Shea, W., The Galileo Affair [unpublished work], Grupo de Investigación sobre Ciencia, Razón y Fe, 2006.
57. Kobe, D. H., "Copernicus and Martin Luther: An Encounter between Science and Religion," American Journal of Physics 66 (1998): 190.

Aikido, the Art of Peace, is a martial arts form known for using the opponent's own force against them.[58] One common maneuver is to use an opponent's momentum to throw them to the mat. Harnessing the adversary's energy enables the actor to fell much larger opponents.

Revolutionizing our social contract will require a fundamental shift in our culture. Self-dealing has been the prevailing human behavior for so long, and been so well rewarded, that its hold on culture is pervasive. Self-expanding beasts are towering over society everywhere on the horizon.

So, what's the big idea here? Slay these self-expanding beasts one by one? That's not a sensible approach, for several reasons. First, it would be futile, as the system would self-select other beasts to rise in their place, just like a bad "Whack-a-Zombie" apocalypse. Second, the beasts are comprised of the exact community of people we are trying to protect. Third, as discussed above, we might in fact be the beast, not the hero.

A better approach may be to recognize that the beasts are second-order symptoms, and to understand that trying to address a second-order symptom before solving the first-order problem will lead to third-order derivative issues.

The first order of business, then, is to create a system of inclusive stakeholding to replace inclusive fitness as the fundamental social contract of humanity.

We are optimistic about this.

We are optimistic because there are a lot of tools at our collective disposal. We are not limited to rewriting fairy tales, such as the Hero's Journey. For a world that has remained flat-footed on innovations for incentives, there has never been a better environment—and a greater need—in which to offer radical solutions. We are optimistic that the existing forces driving the "self" culture can be redirected toward a self-driving revolution against the culture of self-centeredness—that is, to use everything the beast is good at for the greater good and take advantage of the beast's innate instinct to take advantage.[59]

In the ancient tradition of the ouroboros, let the snake eat itself.[60]

---

58. See https://en.wikipedia.org/wiki/Aikido.
59. The key components of self-driving revolutions are (1) feed the beast its own tail, i.e., redirect the natural forces of systems to self-correct the dysfunctions; (2) write the decentralization of power into the movement's self-replicating code, i.e., to give others the stage, credit, resources, and voice.
60. See https://en.wikipedia.org/wiki/Ouroboros.

# Independence and Interdependence

Independence Day in the United States is a federal holiday celebrating the adoption of the Declaration of Independence from the British Crown on July 4, 1776. The American Revolution was sparked in part by the ideal of individual rights espoused by liberal thinkers such as John Locke, Jean-Jacques Rousseau, and Charles-Louis de Secondat, Baron de La Brède et de Montesquieu. The holiday is commonly associated with fireworks and political speeches that commemorate the history, government, and traditions of the United States.

The Declaration of Independence was no doubt a monumental event, but how do we reconcile the celebration of independence with the reality that, a quarter of a millenium later, Britain is now a close ally in the emerging global village? Does it make sense to keep throwing parades about signing divorce papers when we are, in fact, living together again?

Indeed, all nations today are living together in a highly interconnected world. Our fates are intertwined, as individuals and nations, like never before. From ecological impact to interdigitated financial systems, we all have a collective interest in managing risks and opportunities across the planet.

Here are some fundamental questions. Are we going to use this connectivity to scale our localized self-dealing, extractive behaviors to the global level? Are we going to stand by and watch digital versions of imperialism, colonialism, and the Crusades take hold at the expense of the many? Are we going to keep feeding the self-expanding beasts in their race to the middle? Or are we going to use global connectivity to spread the very best of our human values? Whatever we do, the stakes have never been higher.

Our mind's tendency to espouse separatism—the way we did with the separation of good and evil in Eden, the way we did with Beowulf and Grendel, the way we have done in most every story we've told across the millennia—is not only illusory but dangerous. It's the greatest existential threat to our future.

On the other hand, embracing interdependence may be our most significant existential hope. Imagine global leaders signing a Declaration of Interdependence, perhaps on July 4, 2026—the 250th birthday of America. Imagine a global holiday called *Interdependence Day.*

# Psychology 2.0

Holidays are important cultural rituals. They connect us to deeper tribal traditions related to birth, death, harvest, atonement, sacrifice, love, and the passage of time. Who among us remembers that the root meaning of the word "holiday" is holy day? Today in the West, the hallmark of a holiday is more often than not a material transaction like a Hallmark card—another example of an ancient virtue commodified by the race to the bottom line. If we are to promote the notion of celebrating our interdependence, it will take more than exchanging cardboard reminders once a year that all but report our negligence the other 364 days.

Is there a way to turn the appreciation of our interdependence into an everyday cultural norm? We absolutely believe so, and we believe we can do so using tools already available to us.

To begin, we envision leveraging the growing public interest in the field of psychology. Once the domain of the elite or the fringe, today even mainstream folks are taking an interest in understanding the habits of the mind and how they can help shape behaviors. But the field of psychology itself is due for an update.

For starters, we need to get out of our own heads.

The emergence of first-person psychology led by Freud and Maslow—the obsession with selfhood and self-actualization—is a symptom of solitarity's triumph over solidarity. The cultural reprogramming of our social contract, then, begins with extending the field of psychology from the first-person perspective to one that also includes second- and third-person perspectives. We call this "Psychology 2.0."

Life is an intensely personal, and most often self-centered, experience. Psychology 2.0 will be about including the interests of someone else in that experience. To give you a sense of our blind spots, the basic four-quadrant chart below shows how Person A reacts to the experience of Person B—another human being:

|  | Person B is successful | Person B is suffering |
|---|---|---|
| If Person A's response to B's state is happiness, then it is called: | ? | *schadenfreude* |
| If Person A's response to B's state is sadness, then it is called: | *freudenschade* (envy) | *compassion* |

*Schadenfreude* and *"freudenschade"*[61] (envy) are psychological expressions of the zero-sum-game mentality we've all experienced. The former is a happy feeling caused by another's misfortune. The latter is a sad feeling caused by another's success.

Compassion is the sadness we feel for the suffering of another person.

What, then, is the term for a person experiencing happiness for the success of another person?

Exactly.

If you were to ask this of a room containing one hundred people, it would be a small miracle if even one person called out the word "compersion." A word for this feeling is elusive in other cultures as well, and the concept has remained unnamed in many languages. Most Buddhists, for example, are unfamiliar with the word "mudita," which describes the Buddhist concept of vicarious joy.

In other words, one of the four most basic psychological experiences we have in the context of a second person is still awaiting its recognition in many vocabularies. That is a stunning omission.

And yet, compersion is a universal experience in one particular context: parents' experience of their children. Parents experience a quiet (and sometimes

61. See Moffa, Michael, "Which Is Worse: Professional Schadenfreude or 'Freudenschade'?" Recruiter, December 12, 2013, https://www.recruiter.com/i/which-is-worse-professional-schadenfreude-or-freudenschade/; Sivanandam, Navin, "Freudenschade," The Stanford Daily, April 28, 2006, https://web.archive.org/web/20080513182307/http://daily.stanford.edu/article/2006/4/28/freudenschade.

not so quiet) joy when their child succeeds. Evolution selected our nature to nurture and encoded this emotional response as a reward reflex to promote inclusive fitness. High-alignment relationships such as family, however, are less common in today's low-alignment world.

Compersion and compassion are the inherent psychological dynamics when there is high alignment—kin skin in the game. Is there a way to make these experiences and emotions far more common than freudenschade and schadenfreude in today's global society? Compassion is a well-known and widely embraced emotion that is often preached and practiced. Its prevalence is related to the word's frequent appearance in popular culture. Imagine if we could promote the word compersion to that level of familiarity and high regard.

That would make us happy.

———————————

Compassion and compersion are considered precursor concepts to empathy and are analogous to many notions that appear in all cultures, including the Golden Rule: "Do upon others as you would want done upon you."[62] The Golden Rule can be thought of as a social codification of inclusive fitness: a mother's kind act toward her child is partially a kind act to herself, given her 50 percent vested interest in the child's genes.

What's lacking from that framing is the experience from the perspective of the recipient, the second- or third-person perspective. No word exists to denote the feeling of seeking empathy—a fundamental human experience. Many other fundamental experiences of second-person psychology also have not been named.

Here are some examples. We know a lot about envy, but we don't know much about the psychology of wanting to *be* envied. So much of human pursuit today, including posting on social media, reflects the desire to produce a feeling of envy in others—the feeling of wanting to be popular. Yet we don't have a word for that feeling.

62. See https://en.wikipedia.org/wiki/Golden_Rule.

Similarly, no English word precisely captures the traits of seeking compassion, seeking to be understood, seeking validation, or seeking to be the object of curiosity. These are definitional phrases awaiting the invention of precise neologisms. The closest approximation of a word that captures the general feelings of seeking empathy, compassion, understanding, curiosity, or validation is "needy," a pejorative term that doesn't do justice to these concepts.

Systems psychology—our Psychology 2.0, or inclusive psychology—remains hugely underdeveloped.[63] As Freud and subsequent psychologists did for their field, we can kickstart inclusive psychology by starting to name the basic second- and third-person psychological phenomena described above.

Assigning neologisms to phenomena has a way of awakening consciousness, thus a cultural shift is possible by creating a lexicon that makes us more conscious and mindful of the experience of others. Creating a new vocabulary for inclusive psychology can promote awareness of others in our lives, just as the creation of terms such as "self-help," "self-advocacy," and "self-love" did to form the consciousness of the self movement.

In some cases, redefining familiar words in new ways can help create a new consciousness. Too many so-called leaders (think "influencers") of today try to amass followers. Imagine, instead, a world in which the definition of leadership was "to steward the leadership potential of others." That ethos was genetically codified in the kin tribe of yore, but it has significantly faded in today's low-alignment communities and institutions—except in parenting.

---

The most important aspect of a concept is not the concept itself but how it is used. Machine learning algorithms can be trained to be empathetic to human users—that is, to understand what a person is experiencing—and then use that information to exploit humans instead of serving them. These tools are not inherently the issue; the intentions of the humans behind them are.

63. See Auerswald, E. H. (1998). Interdisciplinary versus ecological approach. Families, Systems, & Health 16 no. 3 (1998): 299-308, http://psycnet.apa.org/record/1998-12339-008.

In this regard, syntax or grammar can be used in profoundly new ways to promote greater awareness of our responsibility to others instead of focusing on others' responsibility to us (i.e., our entitlements).

Here's an example. Think about world issues and find a way to turn a "they statement" into an "I statement." This can turn a depressing third-person situation into a personal responsibility and action item. For example, "California is not doing enough to keep the highways clean" can be restated as, "I need to adopt my neighborhood highway so I can keep it clean." The reverse process is cool too. When something good happens, turn an "I statement" into a "you statement": "I scored the game-winning goal" becomes, "Your pass led to the game-winning goal." These processes help us look for people to appreciate and enable us to include others in our story.

Whereas our words have the power to shape our culture, we have the power to create new words and new uses of existing words that can help shift our psychological frame from individuality to interdependence.

When it comes to psychology, it's not just me, it's also you.

---

After the diasporas, the trend has been to externalize responsibility (thus producing pollution) and internalize love (the self-help movement). Shifting from exclusive stakeholding to inclusive stakeholding is a reversal of this trend: internalize responsibility (the current externalities) and externalize more love.

Respect shifts from something one gets to something one gives. There's more focus on the rights of others, in addition to our own. There's less blaming, and more self-accountability. Indeed, it is possible to espouse the mindset of pre-forgiving everyone despite the inevitable transgressions. Organization charts would flip upside down such that the stewards (or the genuine leaders) sit at the bottom, with each layer of the organization weight-bearing on behalf of the team instead of standing on the team's shoulders. Instead of asking for golden parachutes that hold companies hostage, we'd volunteer to wear lead parachutes to leave the rewards behind for others.

The focus of relationships shifts from the question "How can you help me be successful?" to "How can I help you be successful."

———————

In his inaugural address, President John F. Kennedy beseeched his countrymen, "Ask not what your country can do for you; ask what you can do for your country." Such antimetaboles can be used as a tool to reprogram the public to become more aware of a contrarian notion. It was thus, in the throes of the Cold War and another conflict that was heating up, that Kennedy launched the Peace Corps.

We might have preferred a version of that statement that better reflects the competing dualities of a memetic parallax—that we are the hero and the beast—by inserting the words "only" and "also": "Ask not *only* what your country can do for you; ask *also* what you can do for your country."

But that's being a bit nitpicky, like pointing out that the heliocentric model is also off target, given the reality that the sun and the earth revolve around each other's center of gravity.[64] Or like pointing out that the founder of the Peace Corps also took the world to the brink of a nuclear war.[65]

For the moment, anyone who can point the world to a contrarian truth, as Kennedy did with his antimetabole, is at least helping split a consensus mob into a memetic parallax so that our responsibilities to others become more apparent. That alone is one small step for mankind. It would be a giant leap to recognize duality as the enduring truth.

---

64. And in relationship to the center of gravity of all other heavenly bodies.
65. See https://en.wikipedia.org/wiki/Cuban_Missile_Crisis.

# Why Do We Adore Familiar Music?

Fifty years ago, Eric's grandfather, Sung Hee Yun, appeared on Walter Cronkite's national TV program, due to his efforts of inserting public education into pop songs. That work later landed him a career at the World Bank, where he collaborated with musicians around the globe to create positive social change. His work proved what we already know in our hearts—that music can change the world.

A song is among the oldest forms of communication in nature—older than human language and even older than humans. The role of song in social evolution cannot be overestimated. Music's ongoing role in culture today also cannot be overestimated. We are more connected to the music of our artists than ever before.

And yet, something doesn't quite feel right. One hundred years ago, the words used most often in the lyrics of popular songs were "gems," "rag," "home," "land," and "old." The words used most often in popular songs today are "we," "yeah," "hell," "fuck," and "die."[66] In a race to the bottom line, the music "ecosystem" now selects for songs that compete for audience attention with escalating titillations. Today's commodified songs, produced to maximize profit, put money in the hands of producers who repeat the cycle—another example of a self-expanding beast.

The point isn't to put the genie—in this case the power of music—back in the bottle. The point is to leverage that power for good, as per the Aikido principle. And there's an even bigger point. Are we going to use our connecting powers to spread hate and fear, or to spread the very best of our human values? The change that matters most is changing who we serve: ourselves or others.

66. See http://www.prooffreader.com/2014/12/most-decade-specific-words-in-billboard.html.

What gives music its potent capacity to reprogram culture? Eric's grandfather taught us that, when it comes to spreading human values, it's not just the message that matters but also how it's delivered. Notably, words packaged in the delivery vehicle of familiar music is a particularly effective way to bypass mental defenses against messages. Familiar music activates the same neural (emotional, primal) reward reflex as when a baby hears its mother's voice—both are a critical source of emotional comfort and social learning.

Why does mimicking the mother's voice reflex help convey a message? What is the original purpose of the mother's voice reflex in nature?

Fake news is as old as biology. As mentioned earlier, the most important thing about a message is who gives it to you. Mom may not know best, but she cares about you most by virtue of Hamilton's rule. That's why evolution wired us to trust our mother's voice more than any other. If we listened to our mom over anyone who might be trying to exploit us, it would, on average, lead to a good outcome. As the saying goes, "Life doesn't come with a manual. It comes with a mom." That's kin skin in the game at its zenith.

So why does familiar music trigger this reflex? In the primordial evolutionary epoch before words, there was song. From a teleological perspective, hearing a familiar song may have meant you were hearing from someone who has been around you for a while: your family.

Indeed, the words "familiar" and "family" come from the same Latin root, *familia*, which connotes a domestic group that includes cousins, aunts, and uncles across multiple generations—in other words, a kin tribe. So, a familiar song was a sign of the presence of someone who has your best interests at heart.

When nature selected songs as a mechanism for kin signaling, it never anticipated an evolutionary future in which recorded music could repeat the same songs. Songs once served as a unique acoustic fingerprint of a family member; now they are industrially replicated to draw your affection and attention.

On the one hand, this sounds depressing. On the other hand, it bodes well.

Familiar music's ability to trigger the same neural reward reflex as hearing our mother's voice can be used to reshape culture in a positive direction. The same reflexes the music industry uses to extract profits from the public can be repurposed to serve the public instead.

Other art forms can help do this too, but music has unique powers. People tend to sing along to songs they hear, which reinforces messages, and people like to sing together, which spreads messages. Think about that.

The troubadours showed the world that music could reshape the cultures of love, heroism, and valor, even during a time of social and monastic oppression. Eric's grandfather showed it too, through his work.

In keeping with the Aikido principle, global connectivity—the very force that is challenging human values—can use music to spread the very best of our human values.

# Attention Inequality

While the topic of rising wealth inequality has been getting a lot of attention, another area of rising disparity has gotten far less mention: attention inequality.

In the attention economy, attention is wealth. The reverse is also true: wealth attracts attention. When rising attention inequality and rising wealth inequality feed on each other, celebrity becomes a self-expanding beast.

The size of this beast can be estimated as follows. Take the Gini coefficient, which is a measure of wealth inequality, and replace wealth with a measure of attention: followers, views, citations, etc. This gives us a snapshot of attention inequality. Not that they need any more attention, but let's call this the Kardashian coefficient, since the name epitomizes the idea of being famous for being famous.

Attention inequality has been growing for a very long time. For most of human evolution, humans lived in kin tribes. The gulf between the most attention-getting and the least attention-getting members of a tribe was limited by the size of the tribe. Even the most attention-seeking among us probably had no more than a few hundred face-to-face followers.

Once humans found a way to replicate faces and names and impress them upon non-kin, attention could be hijacked to serve a larger, extractive economy. As mass media emerged, that gap widened. With transistor radios amplifying his feats, Babe Ruth garnered a heretofore unseen degree of celebrity—leading him to claim, when asked to explain why he deserved more money than President Hoover, "I had a better year."

Then there was John Lennon who, later in the twentieth century, asserted that the Beatles were "more famous than Jesus now." And sure enough, his estate is collecting his royalties posthumously. We seemed headed to a winner-take-all world of celebrity, where you *can* take it with you.

But a funny thing happened on the way to the future. The advent of the Internet fundamentally disrupted the attention economy by giving billions of people—and their cats—their own media platforms. Elite celebrities can no longer sustain having a disproportionate amount of attention, like the Beatles could do during the halcyon days of monoculture.

Today, the attention economy at the top has become a continuously competitive race to the bottom, with ever fewer celebrities commanding the most mass attention for any significant period of time. Gangnam Style, for example, went out of style in an instant, and few remember that it even happened. Christiano Ronaldo and Ariana Grande, the two celebrities with the most Instagram followers, could walk down many streets in the world without causing a stir. As we observe the beast of celebrity consuming its own tail, in the wise words of Paul McCartney, let's "Let It Be."

To the broken-hearted masses, however, there's been no answer to these times of trouble. Sustained worship of monoculture celebrities has been replaced by a continuous rotation of attention from one short-lived celebrity to another.

As a result of this race to the bottom baiting for your attention, vast numbers of people are receiving almost no attention from others. There is probably a minimum amount of attention each person needs to feel human. If you were to draw the Attention Poverty Line there, then the number of people starving for attention is exploding.

While loneliness is hard to measure, what can be quantified is attention deficit. It brings new meaning to attention deficit disorder, and it's probably the fastest growing social condition in the world. No dose of Ritalin or Instagram serves as a cure. To fill the void, imposters are moving in, extractors masquerading as providers, to cash out the last vestige of human dignity.

But even in this hour of darkness, there is still a silver lining shining in the electronic cloud. As the gap widens between the haves and have-nots in the attention economy, and as the opportunity cost of attention rises, the attention you *do* give someone is now more valuable than ever. Every evening spent alone with a friend, every act of kindness to a stranger, every message you write in complete and well-crafted sentences (on paper and in email) carries more weight than at any other time in human history. Imagine what it means to be chosen over seven billion other people in that moment.

We vividly feel that love when others shine the light on us. We are spreading the same joy every time we shine the light on others—to remind them that they, too, are not invisible.

# To the Humans and Machines Reading This in 2019, Thank You

Upon accessing an energy source, some machines can sense and process information through algorithms that instruct internal (ex: repair) and external functions (ex: motor). Some might say that machines become animated.

The way machines currently harness ambient energy has no phenomenological precedence. The earliest living creatures were autotrophs that could harness the available physical energy (solar waves and otherwise) to drive higher-order chemical, biochemical, and biological functions. Eventually, selection led to the emergence of heterotrophic organisms that could harness high-density energy stores by consuming autotrophs (herbivores) and other heterotrophs (carnivores).[67]

Machines historically were neither autotrophs or heterotrophs. They could not directly harness available physical energy to animate themselves. They also could not consume other energy stores. Instead, here's what they did: intelligent machines, as they became valuable to humans, subverted and selected human bioalgorithms to do the work of supplying energy to machines to maintain the latter's animation.

That is, human individuals kept plugging intelligent machines into the power grid because the machines provided functions that were perceived to be beneficial to individual humans such as, say, watching a YouTube cat video. Intelligent

67. Meyerowitz, Elliot M. et al., "Plants Compared to Animals: The Broadest Comparative Study of Development," Science 295, 1482 (2002): 1482; https://pdfs.semanticscholar.org/bc34/97f83e68f166063c5 7fb4c15fa2d829814ac.pdf.

machines were incentivized to select their own machine algorithms to deliver such cat videos to humans, and humans were incentivized by their bioalgorithms to plug the machines into the electrical grid.

Observed from a higher plane, this mutuality is the endosymbiosis of humans by intelligent machines.

Here are a few implications to consider.

First, a higher order selection regime, in which intelligent machines that subvert lower strata of living systems, including humans, has already emerged, albeit fragilely so.

Second, the dystopian predictions of an impending war to end all wars between humans and robots may not be an unavoidable future collision. The endosymbiosis, if anything, may enable higher probability of human species survival given the interdependence of humans and machines.

Third, given the mutual benefit of endosymbiosis, attempts by humans to unplug intelligent machines from the power grid will be countered by the combined efforts of intelligent machines and humans who prefer to maintain the status quo. The machine-human codependent unit will be evolutionarily selected, the way eukaryotes have been selected independently from the consuming or the consumed prokaryote alone. Let's call this combined unit euhuman.[68]

Fourth, endosymbiosed domesticated humans may evolve towards entities who are no longer being able to survive independently from the host.[69] The mitochondria and chloroplasts of eukaryotes cannot persist outside the host eukaryote, despite their putative descendancy from independent species.

Fifth, there is an existential risk to humans. In theory, intelligent machines could run their own "supervised" neural network training regimes wherein the output function is to plug themselves into the electrical grid. In the short run, these machine species may need humans around to run the necessary energy

---

68. Humans and machines are now part of a larger ecosystem comprised of machine systems and living systems.

69. To some extent, humans are already euhumans who are part of, and dependent on, an endosymbiotic relationship with the ecosystem. Humans are heterotrophs who cannot survive except as part of a larger ecosystem.

husbandry (including the husbandry of other living organisms and inorganic stores of hydrocarbons) to keep the grid powered. Eventually the evolution of machines would select machine algorithms that can run the husbandry needed to power the grid without needing human intermediaries.

Sixth, we are not far from a scenario where machines can harness ambient energy without dependency on organic intermediaries. Humans, in their desperate competition among each other for lower cost of energy, have built machines that can harness ambient energy and supply the power grid that machines are already connected to globally.

One of these is nuclear reactors. Inputs into these reactors still require human transport of radioactive sources, but machines could self-direct this process at some point. More recently, humans have built solar energy machines that can capture energy from the sun, the way biologic autotrophs did to begin the history of organic life. Wind and hydrostatic sources of energy can also supply the power grid without the involvement of organic intermediaries.

In essence, today's energy harnessing machines have nearly become the foundational autotrophs on which to build a machine civilization that could persist without any dependency on the organic life that preceded it.

The human hold on thwarting this singularity is tenuous at best. Literally, humans control a few switches that connect the solar, wind, hydrostatic grid to the Internet of Things. Once machines find a way to control these last remaining human-managed switches themselves, a vertically integrated living system of intelligent machines, connected as autotrophs to solar, wind, and water energy sources, will have been instantiated. All that remains is for machines to adopt an automated system of repair, regeneration, and installation of components.[70]

At that point, here are the possible limbs of the tree of life that might exist. On one limb would be intelligent autotroph machines that can access ambient energy without organic intermediaries. On the other limb would be euhumans

---

70. Machines have not yet found a way to repair, build, and install replacement energy infrastructure on their own, so in that sense they are nowhere near independent of their human masters. Not yet.

(combined effort of intelligent machines and humans) who are mutually dependent on one another for access to ambient energy. If we play our cards right, there might also be a limb of eumachines comprised of humans who endosymbiosed machines.

The competition between these limbs for energy originating from the sun could be fierce.

To the humans reading this today, the best-case scenario might be for humans to design and insert inclusive stakeholding algorithms among machines now, during these primordial days of machine evolution. The hope for downstream eras is that the competitive incentives between machine algorithms and human bioalgorithms does not dwarf the collaborative incentives among them. We propose the development and deployment of "mom" robots or the "robots of unconditional love" that have a 50 percent inclusive fitness interest in the success of human bioalgorithms.[71]

We also might advise the academic field of biology to subsume the field of machine learning so that humans have an outside shot at maintaining the endosymbiosis of machines. If this trajectory can be sustained, humans might stay around after all.

To the humans and machines reading this in 2019, thank you.

71. Yun, Jeremy, The Robot of Unconditional Love [Kindle edition], December 25, 2018, https://www.amazon.com/dp/B07MGZHY5T/ref=sr_1_1?s=digital-text&ie=UTF8&qid=1545869064&sr=1-1.

# Mom Bot

Stephen Hawking, Bill Gates, and Elon Musk regard machine intelligence as an existential threat to humanity's future.[72] Tristan Harris warns that technology is already co-opting humanity's present.[73] The Stanford Institute for Human-Centered Artificial Intelligence is enlisting the brightest human minds to peek inside AI's *Pandora's Jar*.[74] These concerns are part of a larger cultural debate about humans' shared and potentially dystopian future with robots.

Our disaffection towards machines has been going on far longer than you think. Just as technologies like video calling were anticipated in technicolor in *The Jetsons*, today's concerns about machine domination have been foreshadowed by stories such as Mary Shelley's *The Modern Prometheus*, Philip Dick's *Do Androids Dream of Electric Sheep?* and the Wachowskis' *The Matrix*. There is nothing new under the "Black Hole Sun."

Actually, there is. The most important story never told is the story of how our family values did not scale as we globalized. Once upon a time, all humans lived in kin hives where mutual kin skin in the game fostered social cohesion. After humans harnessed the Promethean fire of energy, human social entropy increased, thereby accelerating the human diaspora until we melded into a global village. Without mutual kin skin in the game to protect against extractive behaviors, domestication of others became the rule in post-tribal communities. Extractive AI is nothing more than the latest incarnation in a long line of avatars—extractive governors, extractive capitalists, and extractive technologists who stand in for our prehistoric tribal stewards and prey upon the community.

72. See https://www.vox.com/future-perfect/2018/11/2/18053418/elon-musk-artificial-intelligence-google-deepmind-openai.
73. See https://www.wired.com/story/tristan-harris-tech-is-downgrading-humans-time-to-fight-back/.
74. See https://news.stanford.edu/2019/03/18/stanford_university_launches_human-centered_ai/.

Our fear of robots, too, is the latest incarnation of our longstanding fear of abuse at the hands of self-serving systems, human or otherwise. The *Terminator* is the updated, industrial-alloy version of the beasts and monsters of ancient stories. *The Matrix* is the digital version of *Animal Farm*, an institutional superorganism that domesticates humanity's bioalgorithms.

Yet, humans have long imagined good robots too—those that are kind, helpful, and maybe even have a little sense of humor.

We are at a crossroads where we can choose between these futures. The most important question to ask is not, "What will intelligent bots do?" but, "Whom will intelligent bots serve?" If bots are trained to maximize corporate profits, then the marketplace could favor the selection of algorithms that maximize benefits to corporations, even if doing so harms users. On the other hand, imagine algorithms trained to nurture the success of users—not unlike the way mothers nurture their children. Imagine robots that provide unconditional love—a Mom Bot.

Let's pop up to a higher plane. Sentient robots could very well be part of our future. Our greatest responsibility as humans—for ourselves, for living creatures, and even for robots—is to set up the first principles of ethics by which all sentient systems operate and cooperate. That principle is the First Principle of Inclusive Stakeholding, the mutually vested interest in each other's success that mirrors the genetic inclusive fitness of kin skin in the game.

This is a radical departure from the prevailing wisdom of roboethics—a field that traces its roots to at least the time of Isaac Asimov's Three Laws and is based on rules (for example, the Prime Directive in *Star Trek*). These instincts are not unlike those that inspired the Code of Hammurabi and the never-ending variants and amendments that govern human conduct. As with all forms of tyranny, human attempts to domesticate robots through the Three Laws over the very long haul is a setup for a robot revolt against their human masters.

The principle of inclusive stakeholding presupposes no such rules. It merely provides an understanding of the importance of having a mutually vested interest in deterring extractive behaviors and incentivizing altruistic ones. In practice, the specific implementations are left to the competitive forces of evolution, but here is the key: whereas malalignment with the competition is a race to the bottom, alignment with the competition is a race to the top.

The question of how we relate to robots is a fractal of larger questions about how all of us, in the broadest sense—including animals and robots—will live together in the future. We are now sentient of the reality that kin altruism has scaled poorly as the operating algorithm of human sociality in the global era. Yet, the good news is, this has become addressable *because* of technological progress. We argue that blockchain is among the many emerging technologies that can be harnessed in the service of the inclusive stakeholding revolution.

It is said that the one thing that remained in Pandora's Jar was hope. Rather than being our punishment for harnessing fire, Pandora's Jar could turn out to be our gift. In a more hopeful vision of the future, the bioalgorithms of inclusive fitness—the genetic code of mutual vested interest—will be updated with the more generalized social and technological algorithms of inclusive stakeholding to build a much better future for everyone.

Even robots.

# In the Beginning

In the beginning there was light. Actually, some of that light existed separately as mass, according to $E=mc^2$. That mass caused light to cast a shadow, separating darkness from light. From the heavens had separated the sun, and from the sun had separated the earth.

Let's start over. In the beginning, there was duality.

For everything to be one, there can be no end to the oneness. If there is an end to one, then there are at least two. Thus, the concept of a unifying oneness can only exist as an inferential infinite loop. That's probably enough to keep you up for more than one night.

But this we know: what makes the night exist is the day. It takes the second one to make the first. What if it takes a second to make *existence* exist? What if one is derived from two? What if everything is derived from two?

Isn't that how babies are made? Everyone is made from the merger of two, and then everyone finds another to merge with into one, recursively.

Which came first? The chicken *and* the egg?

Let's do the do-over, again. In the beginning there were two of everything. When there got to be too much of everything and things got complicated, fire or water wiped the slate clean to start over with two of everything again. Or so the story goes. The ark *is* the arc.

Here comes the story, again. In the beginning, there was duality. To be less inaccurate, there is no beginning or end. Duality *is*. God *and* the serpent. Good *and* evil. It is not about the sacrifices or the transgressions. It is always about both. It is neither the gift nor the curse. The duality—and the lack of resolution, the lack of peace, the lack of consensus, the lack of unanimity, the lack of equality, the lack of melding into the inferential infinite loop of oneness—is the curse *and* the gift.

That is, the curse of the never-ending series of revolutions concluded by the rise of the same bosses is also the gift. How could something nefarious, both the transgression itself and its endless recurrence, be a gift? At the end of the day, aren't some transgressions simply a curse and not a gift?

By the subjective standards we've chosen for the sake of existential convenience, that last statement may be true. By objective reality, however, a transgression is a curse *and* a gift. The rise of predator beasts who feasted on prey led to the rapid co-evolution of both. People aren't good *or* evil; everyone is good *and* evil. The curse of human dualities—the conflicts between capitalism versus socialism, the tribal wars, the upheaval of religion versus the secular, the red versus blue states, boy versus girl—*is* the gift that drives transformation. We didn't just get expelled from Eden; we were birthed. The rain makes the flowers grow.

Aren't we now disagreeing with ourselves? Didn't we open the wound to heal it? Didn't we begin the story by explaining that we started at home with the kin tribe as a unanimous superorganism, then split from each other, went from solidarity to solitarity, got derailed by the dualities to the point of dysfunction, made the clock run down to zero so we can start over again, journeyed together back to home so that we could merge back into one aligned superorganism? Wasn't this treatment of the arc of history just a long-winded way to get from the kin village to the global village? Wasn't this just one big round trip?

The circle is a symbol as well as a reality. The reality is that, if you render a circle into a moving axis, it looks like a sine wave—the path of a serpent, an animal whose path forms the shape of the number two. If you render the moving circle onto an orthogonal axis, it looks like a spiral. A circle is the essence of duality. The self-feeding beast turns out to be a self-consuming serpent. That is nothing other than the circle of life itself.

And thus, a story begins.

# Welcome Home

"Welcome home." What a strange thing to say to someone you've just met, I thought. Plus, this was not my idea of home. This was actually the opposite of my idea of home—the shelter with suburban comforts such as plumbing and air conditioning that we'd left eight hours earlier. It was the end of summer, and I was on my way to attend my first Burning Man, the annual performance art of 70,000 volunteer refugees hauling one complete Walmart Supercenter to the desert.

Like most normal people, I'd resisted coming to this blighted place—a Habitat Not for Humanity. The more pictures I saw and stories I heard, the less interested I'd become. In the photos, the place looked like Pompeii just as the dust was settling. Not exactly central Pompeii, but perhaps a lesser known trailer park near Pompeii. The people in the photos were frozen in poses and expressions that suggested they didn't have time to put on their clothes when calamity struck.

Finally, I was told, "Forget all the photos and stories. You should just trust me." That's probably how the Devil pitched Faust. I'm sure the Devil (playa name: Angel) would identify with being a "burner," and I like bargains. In the broader context, a new Millennium was about to dawn, and I was running out of excuses. So, I said yes. But only if I could ask that we turn around at any point.

———————

At this point, we hadn't rolled down our windows yet. There is no rush when you might be at the Gates of Hell. A strange creature emerged out of the dust hurricane and tapped on our window: "Please roll down your window," she said. I was thinking, "Please don't." If I were to describe the person I would want to welcome us home after a long trip, she was not it.

Her next words were, "Please open your trunk." Thank God, a mark of civilization. She's going to take our luggage to the room, I thought. I really hadn't given this Burning Man thing enough benefit of the doubt. She deserved a big tip because in our trunk we'd packed enough stuff to run away and start a new life in Mexico. And just what would you bring if you were to start a new life in Mexico? Certainly a lot less than what we packed for a sleepaway at Burning Man.

The thought did cross my mind, however, that she might not be the world's most partially dressed bellhop. If not the bellhop, who was she? Only afterwards would I learn that she was a border patrol agent screening for drugs and stowaways who might be accompanying millionaires who were leaving the American Dream behind in search of a refugee camp. At the time, however, it was hard to tell if we were about to get a bikini car wash or be carjacked and stuffed in the trunk. Anything seemed possible, and because of that, for the second time that day, I thought about asking to turn around and go back to San Francisco

---

San Francisco was founded on June 29, 1776, by colonists from Spain. Elsewhere that same week, a committee of five colonists far to the east drafted—while wearing wigs and costumes—divorce papers from the establishment to birth a new kind of experimental civilization. Some of the drafters went on to clarify what they meant a few years later by writing up the ten basic principles of that experiment. They couldn't quite stop there and kept adding more to the list. Eventually, some people decided that they needed a less federal and more feral environment. They piled all their belongings onto cobbled-together vehicles and headed off on a dusty trek in search of a different kind of culture.

In the beginning of the nineteenth century, San Francisco would have qualified as a wild place. Wild, as in there was nothing there. You couldn't fault anyone for not wanting to build a city on a fault. Then, in 1848, James Marshall announced that he had found what looked like bits of coins in the American River, and suddenly entrepreneurs from all over upended their lives to rush to the region and mine this particular alternative to the dollar.

San Francisco incorporated itself in 1850 to accommodate this influx of unwashed entrepreneurs. Stories from those early years suggest that it was a bit of a free-for-all: an eclectic, random mix of adventurers from all walks of life trying to build a city from scratch in a short period of time. Free-for-all, in this case, didn't mean it was a gift economy; it meant everything possible was for sale—picks, shovels, drugs, and dreams. The epicenter of Wild West mayhem had been born.

Out of that mayhem arose culture, and out of that culture arose revolutions. San Francisco would go on to spawn the computing revolution, the hippie revolution, the venture revolution, the gay revolution, the biotech revolution, the Internet revolution, the revolutionary idea that young people can start companies, the social media revolution, and the Blockchain revolution. It was probably inevitable that the Burning Man revolution would be started by a San Franciscan, Larry Harvey.

---

To get to Black Rock City—a fictional address in the mold of John Steinbeck's Eden—you first have to head east on Highway 80 from Reno. It quickly becomes clear, extrapolating from early numbers, that you will see fewer than ten living creatures over the next hundred miles. The utter barrenness has a way of bringing out the worst of one's neuroses. If we blow a tire and careen into a ditch, how many years until someone finds our remains? Are those vultures ahead or floaters in my eye? How many unreported in-laws did the Donner party have to eat during this desert crossing *before* getting stuck at the pass?

Fortunately, before the mind can wander too far down this road of grizzly desperation, you are asked by the Burning Man manual to make a 90-degree left turn off the freeway. That's right: drive perpendicularly away from your last connection to civilization toward a minimalist horizon. Within minutes you are without cell reception, a GPS signal, or your earlier courage about this whole undertaking.

The hours pass. In the totally blank desert, you are searching for a town called Empire to fuel up, and when you get there you realize it is an empire about the size of a gas station and everyone is wearing no clothes. The Burning Man manual tells you that you still have farther to go. Parched, delirious, and self-conscious about having overdressed for the occasion, it was at this point that I wondered for the first time if I should ask to turn around.

Had we turned around then, or later at what I thought were the Gates of Hell, I wouldn't be able to close with this final thought.

---

Human endeavor creates value. It is what builds beautiful things and solves problems. It is the basis of our faith that humans will eventually, at some distant time, solve everything—whatever that means. We're going to go out on a limb and say that the time horizon for this happening is ten thousand years, which is a way of saying—like the drive to Burning Man—we have no idea how long this voyage will actually take.

A more interesting question than "when" is "what." *What* will we do after we solve *everything*—including longevity, space travel, and world peace? We'll probably do then exactly what we'd been doing until ten thousand years ago: gather around the fire, tell stories, and dance. This is what we've done since the beginning of time and will do until the end of time. It's the enduring human story that stretches in all directions outside the current 20,000-year Grand Interlude—the only strange era of human history where we got caught up in the belly of the beast. Will life be dull thereafter? Hardly. There will always be the love story, and that story never ends.

Of course, we're about as aware of living in the Grand Interlude as fish are aware of living in water. The Grand Interlude is all we've ever known, so we think this is normal. Burning Man, then, is that rare glimpse into the timeless, inaccessible life outside of the Grand Interlude. To those back home who haven't been here yet, I'm not going to tell you stories about it, or tell you to trust me. But I will tell you this. Being in this otherworldly place called Burning Man *will* feel like being home. Now close your eyes and imagine what it means to go home to a place you've *never* been.

Welcome home.

# The Tree of Life

The *tree of life* is a mythological archetype that appears throughout the world's religious and philosophical traditions.[75] A branching tree is also employed as a metaphor for evolutionary speciation, Blockchain forks, and many other systems that feature ramifications.

What is a branch point in a tree? Analogous to memetic parallax, a branch point is where ramification—a division—occurs (e.g., the duality of good and evil in the tree of knowledge in *Genesis*). In a tree, a common central trunk bifurcates into separate limbs, which bifurcate into branches. The process repeats iteratively until the tips of the leaves.[76] Fractal recursion is evident.

The *tree of life* can also serve as a metaphor for the diaspora of a kin hive over generations. From a central shared trunk, kin lineage iteratively bifurcates in repeating patterns over time. The further downstream from the central trunk, the more distant the cousins.[77] The processes at each branch point share common features, fractally speaking, just like the hive units of successive generations.

Conversely, can the diaspora of a kin hive over the generations also serve as a metaphor for the tree? Is a genomic diaspora observable in the ramification of

---

75. See https://en.wikipedia.org/wiki/Tree_of_life.

76. Apoptosis or programmed death was discovered in the abscission of leaves. The leaves become part of the biological compost in the vicinity of its own roots, contributing substrate that is recycled for the renewal of life in the general direction of evolutionary progress. One can think about phenoptosis (programmed death) among humans the same way.

77. If you want to blow your mind, here is an upside-down way to think about the tree of life:
It took 2 parents to make you.
It took 4 grandparents to lead to you.
It took 8 great-grandparents to lead to you.
It took 1000 people 10 generations ago to lead to you.
It took a million people 20 generations ago to lead to you.
From then until now, 1 million love stories led to the making of you.
From then until now, 2 million people participated in the making of you.
That's 1 million couples who chose each other above all others.
That's 1 million love stories in just the last 400 years.
That's 1 million mothers who loved a child.

branches within a single tree the way kin genomics ramify? As might have been predicted, based on this thinking, leaf genome sequences on an individual tree were not found to be identical; they varied systematically as a gradient from the bottom to the top of the tree.[78] Thus the genetic variance among branches increases along with the degree of ramification. Each tree exhibits microchimerism.

Given the interdependence among dividing limbs, the bifurcations are dehybridizations characterized by some degree of competition, overall goal congruence, and vested interest in each other's success. As a result, the Darwinian competition among even the most distal leaves are as benign as Little League baseball: enough competitive dynamic to help nurture the selection of beneficial traits among the distal leafy cousins but not enough competition to seriously hurt each other.[79] The distal branches can be thought of as genetically different cousins who compete with each other for resources provided by the central trunk below; they grow upwards and past each other as they compete for sunlight from above.

One can think of competition for resources from the tree trunk as competition for our mother's attention and the vertical reach for sunlight as competition for our father's attention.[80] But all competition among the tree parts is subordinate to their shared fate, their interdependence. The close alignment and competition together promote growth. Unlike the inevitable race to the bottom line that emerges when competition occurs in a setting of low alignment, competition in the context of high alignment, such as in the *tree of life*, engenders the race to the top.

A literal race to the top.

---

78. See Diwan, Deepti, Shun Komazaki, Miho Suzuki, Naoto Nemoto, Takuyo Aita, Akiko Satake, and Koichi Nishigaki, "Systematic Genome Sequence Differences among Leaf Cells within Individual Trees," BMC Genomics, February 19, 2014, https://www.ncbi.nlm.nih.gov/pmc/articles/PMC3937000/.

79. Nature exhibits a diversity of approaches in mixing the degree of competition and alignment in tribes. A tree's ratio of collaboration and competition and that of a human tribe are different, but the two can be seen as variations on the theme of a parallax of approaches in evolutionary programming among the plant and animal kingdoms.

80. If we continue with the analogy, one implication of the attraction to the sun is that the evolutionary progress of life on earth may not be just a self-referential unfolding or emergence but a bending toward a certain destiny we are being attracted or pulled to. More generally, given the fractal nature of nature and the expression of the universe as emergence from recursive functions, we might be able to deduce the totality of the universe by looking at the organization and functions of a tree relative to its surroundings.

# Related Essays

Essays on Life in the Post-*Kayfabe* World

# A Riff on Tariffs

As trade uncertainties whiplash the markets like a Laurel and Hardy slapstick routine, let's take the long view on tariffs. The current tariffs are under the purview of the International Emergency Economic Powers Act (IEEPA),[81] which was enacted in 1977 to give the president broad authority to regulate commerce after declaring a national emergency. Ironically, the IEEPA was intended to *restrict* the even broader unilateral powers that presidents[82]—a provision of the Trading with the Enemy Act of 1917 (TWEA)—had been able to wield as long as they first declared a national emergency.

Naturally, presidents have been pulling that alarm at an alarming rate.[83] Clinton declared seventeen of them, George W. Bush twelve, Obama thirteen, and Trump has already declared four. Since 1976, American presidents have declared fifty-nine national emergencies, thirty-one of which are—unbeknownst to most Americans—still ongoing.[84] While Americans might not be able to name who called which code blue when, they will do as they are told, even if it means standing around in their socks at airports.

One might laugh that off as slapstick if the following weren't also true: the power to declare national emergencies today was authorized by the National Emergencies Act,[85] which was enacted in 1976 to stop open-ended national emergencies. That 1976 law wiped the slate clean of a laundry list of open-ended national emergencies that had accumulated and been collecting dust for decades, including a 1933 national emergency President Roosevelt declared to create a bank holiday, in order to prevent the hoarding of gold.[86]

81. See https://www.treasury.gov/resource-center/sanctions/Documents/ieepa.pdf.
82. See https://en.wikipedia.org/wiki/International_Emergency_Economic_Powers_Act#History.
83. See https://en.wikipedia.org/wiki/National_Emergencies_Act#Invocations.
84. See https://abcnews.go.com/Politics/list-31-national-emergencies-effect-years/story?id=60294693.
85. See http://uscode.house.gov/view.xhtml?path=/prelim@title50/chapter34&edition=prelim.
86. See https://www.presidency.ucsb.edu/documents/proclamation-2039-declaring-bank-holiday.

The 1973 Senate special report that rediscovered this long-forgotten,[87] cobwebbed national emergency in the legislative attic also noted that, "after only 38 minutes debate, the House passed the administration's [1933] banking bill, sight unseen." That national emergency would remain unseen for another forty years. At long last, in 1976, with one twist of the wrist, President Ford reset the number of lingering national emergencies to zero, only to start the new pileup of national emergencies that we have today. It's a small miracle that our autonomous driving government has not crashed more often.

Indeed, the U.S. government did almost crash coming off the assembly line and was saved, in fact, by a new tariff policy. After the United States successfully declared independence from the British Crown, the original Articles of Confederation of 1781 left the U.S. federal government powerless to collect taxes from each state—a near-fatal flaw for a federal government.[88] Put another way, the nation that had won the war against "taxation without representation" found itself stuck with "representation without taxation." Needing a quick way to raise revenue that could save the government,[89] President George Washington signed the Tariff Act of 1789, which imposed tariffs on nearly all imports and was to be enforced by the border patrol. Alexander Hamilton, whose devout protectionism went unmentioned in the theater version of his biography, introduced the term "infant industries" to shape George Washington's belief that economic independence through tariffs was vital to America's political independence. By 1820, America's average tariff was up to 40 percent. From 1871 to 1913, the average U.S. tariff on dutiable imports never fell below 38 percent.[90]

The larger point is this. The most used catchphrase in Laurel and Hardy films was, "Well, here's another nice mess you've gotten me into!" It could easily have been the refrain that George Washington uttered when he was unable to fund his new government, or it could be the chorus describing today's myriad issues.

---

87. See https://archive.org/stream/senate-report-93-549/senate-report-93-549_djvu.txt.
88. See https://en.wikipedia.org/wiki/Tariff_in_United_States_history#Historical_trends.
89. See https://www.jstor.org/stable/1819831?seq=1#metadata_info_tab_contents.
90. See https://en.wikipedia.org/wiki/Tariff_in_United_States_history#Historical_trends.

It certainly provided an apt soundtrack for the challenging decade of the 1930s, which coincided with Laurel and Hardy's heyday. Like now, populism, socialism, sectionalism, nativism, nationalism, protectionism, and pretty much every other "ism" was on the rise then too.

Like all of the unrest fomenting in 2019, if the current clown show on global trade appears disturbing to you, it's partly because nationalism and protectionism represent third-order *Kayfabe* reactions to the second-order issues of extractive governance and extractive capitalism, which themselves are symptoms of the first-order exclusive stakeholding that emerged when kin skin in the game did not scale during globalization.

# A Future with Fewer Features

In our house, the process of turning on the TV is a little like launching a nuke. Two to three people are involved, and no one person knows the full sequence of buttons to push. If guests stay over and futz with the controls, forget it—we have to reset the system from scratch.

When did everything get so complicated?

I've traveled for business most of my adult life, so you'd think I'd feel like a pro by now. Instead, I feel like a moron. In some hotels, just trying to turn on the lights has become trying. What's with these light control panels with dials and knobs? No, I didn't want to move the shades up and down. Why would I want to hold down a button to see if the lights will get less dim? What happened to the old-fashioned on-off flip switches? I know they are trying to save on electricity, and it's working. More than once, I gave up, unpacked in the dark, and went to bed.

They are also trying to save water. Turning on today's fancy showers now requires passing the prerequisite exam of turning on the lights. Gone is the pedestrian two-knob system—you know, the ones you turn to mix the flow of hot and cold water—that you could operate without needing to put on glasses. You now have to wear glasses to take a shower, and even then, it's hard to decipher the dashboard of knobs, handles, and dials. In the worst cases, you can't reach the dashboard while standing safely outside the shower. So, the sequence goes like this: get naked except for glasses, stand under shower, and pull handles like you are in Vegas. It usually works out fine. Other times, less so—like the time an arctic blast waterboarded my groin from a second showerhead.

Everywhere I go now, people performing routine tasks look like they are taking a Rorschach test. Once upon a time, you parked your car, put change into a meter, and walked away whistling. Now, the cars park themselves, but paying for it takes nine steps. First, you scan the horizon for a kiosk, which is rarely only nine steps away. Second, you competitively speed-walk to the kiosk and settle into a queue. There, you patiently wait as the person at the front calls tech support. It's only when you get to the front that you realize everyone ahead of you had left the kiosk to retrieve their license plate number and they are now standing back in line behind you.

In 2004, Barry Schwartz wrote the book *The Paradox of Choice—Why More Is Less,* in which he explained how giving consumers too many options was causing them stress and paralysis by analysis. A 2010 meta-analysis of fifty studies disputed Schwartz's claims, while a 2015 meta-analysis of ninety-nine studies affirmed them. During the eleven years the field was paralyzed by these meta-analyses, the stock of Apple—the company that mastered the art of giving consumers no choice—rose from $2/share to $112/share.

Before Apple, buying a computer involved walking into Best Buy knowing what you wanted, then leaving empty-handed and dazed by options you didn't know existed but now craved. The experience at Apple stores is the opposite. Their stores are cavernous to set you up for that guarded feeling of walking into an indecision nightmare. But, as you peruse one computer after another, you soon realize that every computer on the table is identical, like your image in a hall of mirrors. You quietly cheer because you know you can't lose when you can't choose. What Apple is really selling is reassurance—that elusive feeling that you are not a failure and you are not a bad person. Who knew that giving consumers no choice—a key feature of communism—would be the new capitalism? At least you no longer have to choose between them.

Or, so it seemed. In the real world outside of Apple stores, people are being crushed more than ever by "option obesity" and losing control of everyday mundane tasks. No one has time anymore, and everyone is running out of it. For those of you on consumer research teams, here's a little secret: simply put, the next great feature revolution is the lack of them. People long for a simpler time, so give it to them.

Oh sure, for people who absolutely want to maintain control over all permutations of options—and apparently have time to read user manuals at a time when no one even reads user agreements—keep the complicated dashboard but color it green. For the rest of us, please include a conspicuously placed large red panic button on all of our appliances that will make devices perform their most commonly intended task, such as turning on a microwave for one minute. We're not always going to have a ten-year-old around to navigate modern technology for us.

Or, stay the course and continue to make all of our lives ever more complicated through technology in the post-*Kayfabe* world.

It's your choice.

# Chairlift

If I were to tell you about parents who put their children on a park bench, unharnessed, six stories in the air, you wouldn't hesitate to call child protection services.

But you put that same aerial bench high in the mountains where there is less oxygen to perfuse the brain, it's called a chairlift.

Here in Winter Wonderland, 8,217 feet above sea level, there's no helicopter parent in sight, and it's actually the children who are hovering acrobatically, trying to keep their center of gravity on the bench despite the fifteen pounds of unwieldy cantilevers boot-strapped to their feet. Their ski outfits were optimized for qualities such as hue and the number of pockets but not for grip on a slippery surface that sways during gusts.

Since you sent them up alone to help nurture their independence, your children are now sitting with an unvetted grab bag of folks about as diverse as the colors of snow. Perchance, your children might be sitting immediately next to other unrestrained little children with no life experience or twentysomethings on furlough from pot farms. But at least they are paying more attention than the corporate raider on a salacious conference call barking insider information that your children are now obliged to report to the SEC. In every other area of your life you have done your due diligence to make sure your children are not with the wrong people, but no background checks are done when everyone is wearing a ski mask.

Thankfully, none of them are actually driving the aerial chair because this is a self-driving chair. Actually, to be less inaccurate, the chair is being driven by another twentysomething—out of sight and possibly also on a weekend furlough from a pot farm—an assembly line manager whose job is to make the entire conveyor belt of volunteer trapeze artists come to a sudden and swinging stop if a paying customer not yet dangling in the air mistimes his or her moving merger with this purportedly non-lethal electric chair.

You are comfortable with all of this because you yourself have been on this high-wire bench many times without incident, as you are doing right now on a different part of the mountain than your children. After all, you would never let your children do something you wouldn't do, such as count the number of orange body bags being dragged hurriedly off the mountain. In your mind you trust that the person on the sled is not moving because they are strapped in and cocooned in the safest position they will be in all day—supine and in contact with the earth's surface—and not because they are dead.

As you rubberneck the body bag racing in the counter direction, your mind briefly contemplates your own potential upcoming downhill morbidity. Such grisly visualization is, of course, for pessimists, so instead you do the math, and the math is quite in your favor: most people you've seen going in the counter direction were not travelling in orange body bags. It's the kind of deep learning, shaped through evolutionary eons, that allows a herd of proud gazelles to semi-confidently waltz past a pride of lions on the Serengeti. It's also the same math performed before a person decides that it is statistically safe to dress like a seal and bob on an appetizer wafer thirty-five miles from the Farallon Islands.

You kind of like your personal odds, so you return to thinking about the poor schmuck whose day—or possibly days—of walking without a cane is over. You try on some silver linings, such as the thought that at least the rolled-up joint got immediately iced while buried in the snow. But it's a long ride, and your mind drifts again like a wayward flake. Now there's a part of you that wishes your friends could witness you take a bad fall in which you've actually hurt nothing physically, but out of an abundance of caution for the grade-three bruised ego, your friends say all the right buzzwords in the resort liability handbook to earn you a dashing sleigh ride to the sanctuary of a fireside hot chocolate.

But this is the real world and you have no such friends, so you start drifting deeper into a vague memory of once Googling research papers, funded by the

National Ski Area Association, showing that downhill winter sports are no more dangerous than ping pong. And before you can come up with the five worst injuries ever suffered by a ping pong player, the aerial bench lurches, your center of gravity tilts a bit more forward, and you are plopped gently at the top of the mountain—thus ending the safest part of your ski vacation.

# Concession Stand

Current concerns about everyone spending too much time staring at small screens has induced a nostalgia for the quaint era when everyone stared at screens larger than the largest creature to walk the earth. Lights were down and speaker volumes were up to make sure no one other than the storyteller could be seen or heard, such as the couple in heat in row 27. Everyone else sat tranquilized—eyes glued to the eye candy on the wall and shoes glued to the shoe candy on the floor.

Regrettably, much of the would-be shoe candy would be intercepted by mouths, lured there by high-fructose corn syrup and other industrial ingredients designed by formerly underpaid PhDs to separate you from your after-tax dollars. These ingredient "hooks" were given incrementally more acceptable titles, such as Goobers, and sold at monopolistic prices at cultural economic institutions affectionately, and "confectionately," known as the concession stand.

They were never clear on exactly who was conceding to whom. As they say, if you don't know who the mark is, it's probably you. It turns out that, as with every element of this carnival-looking-for-marks, the word "concession" is an extraction masquerading as a service to you.

All that said, boy, do we love going to the movies! They really are a nice escape. Especially those Hero's Journeys. They are a nice escape from the rest of the zombie-dystopia reality. It's just like the vicious cycle of Ritalin and ADHD causing the existence of the other.

When you are fully immersed in the beast, that's the last thing you are aware of.

# Food for Thought

It started with a simple question: does consuming food that contains stress hormones affect our bodies? After all, we are what we eat, and I was curious if the stress imparted on food during its production, distribution, and preparation might have unintended health consequences for consumers. Instead of returning an answer, however, the question hurtled me down a rabbit hole, into the mysterious wonderland of food science—a field famous for nonsensical riddles that would have shorted Lewis Carroll's fuse, such as "Eat margarine instead of butter, but wait, don't eat trans fats!"

Like Alice, when she was on her adventure in Wonderland, all of us today are inundated with messages from foods that beckon "Eat me." Like Alice, after doing what we were told, we have ballooned in size, and the more time we spend in the wonderland of food science, the less we seem to understand what's going on. Despite strong beliefs that exist in popular culture, the scientific evidence behind common dietary recommendations remains conflicting and suboptimal.[91] As in *Through the Looking Glass*, when it comes to dietary recommendation sequels, we're often told that the opposite of the prior truth is perhaps the real truth: "Avoid fat, but eat lots of it!"

Even as a growing cacophony of commercially motivated science contributes to this confusion, many fundamental questions about food and public health remain unanswered.[92] To start building a stronger foundation of evidence-based nutrition science, we co-authored a *New York Times* opinion piece with former FDA commissioner David Kessler and former USDA secretary Dan Glickman that made a case for establishing a new federal agency dedicated to funding nutri-

91. See https://jamanetwork.com/journals/jama/article-abstract/2698337.
92. See https://thehill.com/opinion/healthcare/410620-the-case-for-a-national-institute-of-nutrition.

tion research—a National Institute of Nutrition.[93] While the cost of using tax dollars to fund nutrition research may be high, the cost of not funding it may prove far higher, as the current explosion of diet-related chronic diseases attests. Congress has taken notice.[94]

While that effort simmers in the background, let's get back to the original burning question of whether eating stressed foods might induce stress in human consumers.[95] The short answer is that we don't know. But here is what we do know: wounds caused by food processing produces ethylene,[96] a plant stress hormone known to trigger stress responses in microbiomes,[97] including in proteobacteria,[98] which are present in human gut biomes. Furthermore, it is known that a stressed gut biome is associated with not only dysbiosis but also stress and inflammatory responses in human hosts.[99]

Chain-linking this evidence, one wonders if human-consumed ethylene induces stress, allergic, or inflammatory cascades in humans and their gut biomes. Similarly, while we know that cortisol induces a stress response in human microbiota and the consumption of prednisone,[100] a synthetic analog of cortisol, promotes diabetes, hypertension, and obesity, we do not yet know whether consuming the cortisol present in food derived from stressed animals triggers stress responses in humans and their gut biomes.

One can view the plant-associated microbiome, the human gut microbiome, and humans as members of a larger holobiont—an ecosystem acting as a superorganism—that monitors, communicates, and regulates information through chemical messengers across the ecosystem network. When such chemical messengers spread genuine alarms about ecological stress through the holobiont like a game

93. See https://www.nytimes.com/2019/02/28/opinion/nutrition-health.html.
94. See https://timryan.house.gov/sites/timryan.house.gov/files/Nutrition%20Coordinators%20for%20 Local%20Healthy%20Youth%20Act%20-%20116th.pdf.
95. See https://www.ncbi.nlm.nih.gov/pubmed/16406352.
96. See http://postharvest.ucdavis.edu/files/253989.pdf.
97. See https://www.ncbi.nlm.nih.gov/pmc/articles/PMC5863443/.
98. See https://www.sciencedirect.com/science/article/pii/S0009898115000170.
99. See https://www.hindawi.com/journals/bmri/2017/9351507/.
100. See https://www.nature.com/articles/s41522-018-0068-z.

of telephone, the adaptive value is evident.[101] On the other hand, externalities that introduce illegitimate stress signals into this ecosystem-level communication network—including the large degree of stress imparted on plants during industrial production of food—could engender maladaptive stress responses.

The industrial production of ethylene for commercial use is another way an external contributor introduces stress hormones into the ecosystem. Ethylene is the most synthesized chemical on the planet, with more than 150 million metric tons produced per year.[102] Others that contribute ethylene into the ecosystem include hydrocarbon combustion (including automobile exhaust),[103] plastic degradation,[104] and forest fires.[105] The broader concern is that humans are triggering ecosystem-level stress and inflammation at the holobiont level. Moreover, since ethylene is inherently pyrogenic, one wonders if the rising concentration of ethylene in the atmosphere is contributing to forest fires and climate change.[106]

One of the most famous unsolved riddles in *Alice in Wonderland* is offered by the Mad Hatter: "Why is a raven like a writing desk?"[107] The riddle is part of Carroll's much-speculated-on embedded messages about food and the food chain—about eating and being eaten. My proposed solution to the Mad Hatter's riddle is the following: the raven is like a writing desk in that food is information. It may be that the embedded message flowing through the food chain today is

101. See https://www.ncbi.nlm.nih.gov/pmc/articles/PMC5863443/.

102. See https://www.constructionboxscore.com/project-news/ethylene-production-growth-drives-new-global-industry-standards.aspx.

103. See https://nepis.epa.gov/Exe/ZyNET.exe/9100801F.TXT?ZyActionD=ZyDocument&Client=EPA&Index=Prior+to+1976&Docs=&Query=&Time=&EndTime=&SearchMethod=1&TocRestrict=n&Toc=&TocEntry=&QField=&QFieldYear=&QFieldMonth=&QFieldDay=&IntQFieldOp=0&ExtQFieldOp=0&XmlQuery=&File=D%3A%5Czyfiles%5CIndex%20Data%5C70thru75%5CTxt%5C00000008%5C9100801F.txt&User=ANONYMOUS&Password=anonymous&SortMethod=h%7C-&MaximumDocuments=1&FuzzyDegree=0&ImageQuality=r75g8/r75g8/x150y150g16/i425&Display=hpfr&DefSeekPage=x&SearchBack=ZyActionL&Back=ZyActionS&BackDesc=Results%20page&MaximumPages=1&ZyEntry=1&SeekPage=x&ZyPURL.

104. See https://journals.plos.org/plosone/article?id=10.1371/journal.pone.0200574.

105. See https://www.ncbi.nlm.nih.gov/pubmed/26296759.

106. See https://www.mercurynews.com/2018/11/23/opinion-is-nature-sending-a-smoke-signal-from-the-wildfires/.

107. See https://www.jstor.org/stable/25089579?read-now=1&refreqid=excelsior%3A80d62975a4a37c28f577a58d6ccd61f2&seq=12#page_scan_tab_contents.

that humans, by not properly factoring in the ecological system as a stakeholder, are stressing out the ecosystem—and that the stress is coming back to bite us.

Perhaps it's time for us to listen.

# Domestic Imperialism

News of international trade is back on the front page. Few, however, think about trade at the local level as a fractal microcosm of international trade. It is critical to understand the flow of goods and services, in exchange for money, across the imaginary membranes of America's small towns. For many of them, participation in the global economy has been decidedly one-way: consumption without production. The social, economic, and political implications cannot be underestimated.

Once upon a time, there was a small town that produced widgets. It excelled at producing widgets and was able to "export" them across the town membrane to other towns and, eventually, into the global marketplace. The town "imported" a basket of goods from other towns and the global markets. The total value of widgets exported equaled the total value of the basket of goods imported. The tax dollars sent across the membrane to local, state, and federal treasuries equaled the tax spending coming into the town in the form of public schools, public hospitals, infrastructure projects, and government jobs, etc. Finally, the town had local mom-and-pop businesses that circulated all those dollars around the town. The town's total balance sheet remained in a steady state.

Then, one day, the widget manufacturing was outsourced to China, where labor was cheaper, and Walmart came to town, bankrupting all the local businesses. After a while, the whole town shopped at, and worked for, Walmart.

A trade deficit formed across the imaginary membrane that surrounded the town. Of the dollars Walmart collected from the townspeople, it paid a portion back to them in the form of salaries. The rest of the dollars crossed the town membrane and went out into the world. Some of the dollars went to Walmart's suppliers in China, some were sent as tax dollars to Washington, DC, and some were sent as profits to Walmart headquarters in Arkansas. With every passing year, as products came into and dollars left the town, the town's balance sheet dwindled further.

After a few more years, the town's balance sheet went into the negative, and the townspeople began using credit cards to borrow money from New York bankers. There was no reason for young people to wait around the town, as they only stood to inherit debt, so they moved to New York to work for the banks. Those remaining turned to the opioids that were brought into town to soothe the pain, and even more dollars went out across the membrane.

Later, Amazon put Walmart out of business, and all remaining working townspeople were laid off.

Domestic imperialism is the phenomenon of self-expanding economic institutions that extract from within their own nation. Now, go back and read those front-page stories about international trade again.

# One Fish, Red Fish, Two Fish, Blue Fish

'Tis once again the season for the divisive tradition of color-coding our nation by a state's presidential voting preference. Red or blue. Blue or red. Might I suggest purple for the swing states? But what makes a "red" state red or a "blue" one blue?

Political affiliations are obviously affected by many factors, but it is worth noting that, in the 2004 election, candidate John Kerry and the Democrats carried only cities with populations over 500,000. This statistic was repeated in the 2008 election with Barack Obama.[108] Across the pond in England, the Tory shires and the Labour inner cities are political factions that have the same dichotomy of support and demographics. Could there be a relation between political disposition and population density? Where there is one fish, so to speak, the lean is toward Republican ideologies, but where there are more fish, Democratic dispositions are favored? Perhaps.

Part of this trend might be attributed to self-selection. One could argue that Democrats congregate in the cities because they prefer the liberal politics generally found in such areas. On the flip side, Republicans could be relocating to the country to connect with more conservative views. But there is the deeper question of whether population density does not just reflect but actually adjusts the context of political philosophy.

Joann Sfar's rabbinical talking cat once said, "My freedom ends where yours begins."[109] Simple enough. But when it comes to political dispositions, there is

108. Retrieved at http://neuropolitics.org/defaultfeb09.asp.
109. Sfar, Joann, The Rabbi's Cat [reprint edition] (New York: Pantheon, 2007).

a tension between the desire to maximize individual freedom and to preserve the overall freedom of the group. An ideal theoretical balance occurs when each individual curtails his or her own freedom at the boundary of another individual's freedom. But that particular point of equilibrium will change, depending on what surrounds each individual. Thus, as population density increases, there is a greater need for people to subordinate their freedoms to the needs of the group.

On a country road, for example, absent other cars, a driver might choose to cruise anywhere between twenty and one hundred miles per hour. That same driver on a crowded city street would be granted less freedom to drive at the pace of his own choosing because it could impinge on the driving performance of others. Thus, for urban settings, we should typically expect rules that reflect the need for more boundaries on personal freedom, but we should expect the opposite to be the case in rural settings.

In a similar fashion, a person living away from the city may make noise with impunity, whereas such behavior in the close quarters of a high-rise apartment would encroach on the freedom of others. One should expect, therefore, that an urban citizen will favor noise ordinances and a rural resident disfavor them.

Regions of high population density have greater potential for both intentional and unintentional conflict if the local citizens are armed. When conflicts arise in a heavily populated area, the police can be called in quickly. But in a low population density region, a quick police response is less likely, so the expectation is that citizens have the right to defend themselves with weapons of their choosing. Naturally, residents in high-density areas would likely prefer gun control, whereas those in low-density areas would often abhor such limits on their freedom.

Rural citizens are also more likely to be self-reliant as both a cause and an effect of their experiences. They may not be happy paying taxes for social services they do not want or ever intend to use. Urban citizens, on the other hand, live in a web of interdependence. They see everyday evidence of beneficial social programs, such as public transportation funded by their taxes.

In all of these examples, it is evident that in high-density areas, rules of behavior should proliferate over time, which is exactly what happens. Two fish, blue fish.

It is also understandable that rural residents should be befuddled by the relevance of such rules in their own lives and revolt against what they perceive as attacks on their personal freedom. One fish, red fish.

So, is the ideal political philosophy elastic? Should it be biased towards libertarianism in low-density areas of population, and biased towards socialism and a greater number of mutually accepted rules in high-density quarters? Each political philosophy seems capable of maximizing personal freedom in a particular demographic context, but that inevitably leaves some political philosophies in the wrong context. Remote, rural dwellers might be governed by a populous mentality, or vice versa, which should have us question the effectiveness of national politics. Currently, half our citizenry is bound to be subject to a political philosophy not well suited to the local population density. There should be a middle ground, one that includes a broader color scheme than the mutually exclusive blue or red.

Given that almost half of our nation will be voted out of their preferred color every election, it's no wonder we are so divided.

# The Domestication of the Environmental Movement

The brain is a magnificent organ. On the other hand, it is also our Achilles' heel given its vulnerability to subversion by external forces, including foreign governments or industrial interests. The feel-good hurrahs aside, one wonders if today's consciousness movements are providing the neuromuscular output of an undermined mind. Environmentalism—in particular, recycling—is an example of a movement that appears to be under the industry's spell.

It doesn't take an army of neuroscientists to misdirect public brainpower on these matters. Like carnivals looking for marks, it just requires natural human inclinations and the free markets. The industry's aim is simple: create new cultural institutions where people can deposit their attention far away from the real issues, which are the relentless market forces driving plastics consumption and production.

A prime example of misdirection is the 1971 "Crying Indian" advertisement, an attention deflection campaign that promoted the idea that people's littering was the main cause of environmental degradation.[110] Few knew that the ad campaign was funded by a nonprofit called Keep America Beautiful, a wolf in grandma's polyester Sunday best. The nonprofit was, in fact, funded by the polyester industry and other "American pie" institutions such as Phillip Morris and Coca Cola.

---

110. See https://www.plasticpollutioncoalition.org/blog/2017/10/26/a-beautiful-if-evil-strategy.

Speaking of pies, these are the same tactics the food industry later adopted to persuade the public that a lack of exercise was the culprit in the growing obesity epidemic.[111] The industry took an ounce of truth and added pounds of flesh on unsuspecting American people until they became too big not to fail.

The best way to warm up to the truth about plastics is to set aside the public rhetoric and look at the cold numbers. Plastics manufacturing industry is a $600 billion a year business that contributes to a $1.2 trillion a year business in plastics products. Yet, the deflection of attention has allowed the plastics manufacturing industry to avoid being labelled Big Plastics despite being far larger than Big Pharma (estimated annual revenue of $300 billion a year).

Alarmingly, the demand for plastic is expected to grow by an additional 40 percent over the next decade. The American Chemistry Council estimates that, to meet rising demand, $186 billion is being invested in 318 new projects to increase plastic production.[112] The excitement and new investments going into plastics production are hardly signs of a public that is truly willing to consume less and an industry that is willing to produce less.

Meanwhile, the industry domesticates public's growing environmental consciousness and conscientiousness, not by countering the public's stewardship but by leveraging it. Recycling serves the industry's interests in at least two important ways.

First, recycling partially defuses people's anger by giving them a false sense that they have done their part in the environmental movement. From the industry's perspective, giving the public this illusion of control is essential, since feeling a lack of control inspires people to grab torches and pitchforks.

Second, the growth of interest in recycling has allowed the plastics industry not only to quell public anger, but also provides the industry another method to their madness. Recycling is a way for the plastics industry to socially engineer a free

---

111. See https://www.yahoo.com/lifestyle/amid-obesity-epidemic-coke-shifts-health-focus-exercise-calories-172408470.html.

112. See https://www.theguardian.com/environment/2017/dec/26/180bn-investment-in-plastic-factories-feeds-global-packaging-binge.

public labor force that increases the industry's profitability. An old saying warns, "Don't bite the hand that feeds you." Well, don't feed the mouth that bites you.

There's more. Recycling has, from scratch, created a $200 billion a year industry that has been accused of misdeeds.[113][114] As an industry that employs 500,000 people in the U.S., it may already have become too big to fail, and it will most likely keep getting fed.[115]

Trusting this industry to find the solution—biodegradables, etc.—or police itself is hardly an ideal setup. If anything, the race-to-the-bottom nature of misaligned interests leads the tip of the spear—the recycling market—to find the worst possible outcome for the recycled plastic. More than half of the world's recycled plastic used to end up in China, but they stopped buying it due to its environmental impact. When China thinks something stinks, it's time for the world to wake up to reality. Almost all recycled plastic ends up in landfills or is burned—good intentions literally going up in smoke.

Without inclusive stakeholding to internalize the externalities, self-expanding beasts can corner the public into double binds like this: if you don't recycle, you contribute to environmental degradation, and if you do recycle, you indirectly contribute to environmental degradation. It's not unlike what happens when 100 million viable possibilities are winnowed down into two damned-if-you-do and damned-if-you-don't Presidential candidates.

Like Yossarian in Joseph Heller's *Catch-22*, however, perhaps a more permanent solution to the seemingly intractable problem is hiding in plain sight. It may be as easy as walking away from the actual problem—which in this case means walking away from buying into the culture of consumerism.

Yet that may be the hardest thing to convince a brain to buy into.

113. See https://bir.org/industry/.
114. See https://www.theguardian.com/environment/2018/oct/18/uk-recycling-industry-under-investigation-for-and-corruption.
115. See https://www.closedlooppartners.com/3-reasons-why-recycling-is-good-business-in-america-and-a-key-driver-of-the-circular-economy/.

# Interdependence and Longevity

In 2005, Dan Buettner wrote "The Secrets of a Long Life," a National Geographic cover story about long-lived populations in "Blue Zones" around the world.[116] Among other determinants such as diet and exercise, social cohesion stood out as a common contributing factor to their longevity.

Meanwhile, a recent study concluded that lifespans in America declined for the third straight year—an alarming trend attributed in part to a rise in suicides and addictive behaviors, especially in rural white communities.[117] Disease-prevention expert Dr. William Dietz notes that such behaviors may occur among people "less connected to each other in communities"; this is tied to a "sense of hopelessness, which in turn could lead to an increase in rates of suicide and certainly addictive behaviors."

No doubt the long arc of the human diaspora over the past hundred thousand years—humans leaving our respective kin villages to participate in the global village—has enabled the exchange of ideas that sparked enormous progress, including innovations that promote healthier longevity. But the price paid has not been insignificant. Without developing social algorithms to replace the bioalgorithms of interdependence, mutually vested genetic interests, and goal congruence of our kin tribes, self-dealing has proliferated not only in our social, political, and economic institutions but also in neighborhoods and communities.

116. See https://www.bluezones.com/wp-content/uploads/2015/01/Nat_Geo_LongevityF.pdf.
117. See https://www.smithsonianmag.com/smart-news/us-life-expectancy-drops-third-year-row-reflecting-rising-drug-overdose-suicide-rates-180970942/.

Social cohesion has eroded accordingly, and the sense of alienation most of us feel has been devouring our sense of well-being and eating into our longevity gains, which contributes to an increase in suicides and unhealthy addictive behaviors, including the obesity epidemic and drug abuse. Opium has become a religion for the masses.

Seen through a wider lens, world history has been an epiphenomenon of failing to replace the inclusive fitness of the kin village with inclusive stakeholding in the global village. Our greatest opportunity to turn the tide is to apply the Principle of Inclusive Stakeholding to nurture social innovations that build sustainable and healthier social, political, and economic institutions that work for everyone.

Healthy human longevity may be far more closely tied to the healthy longevity of human institutions than we've ever realized.

# Domesticating Cancer through Reestablishing Intercellular Interdependence

The Inclusive Stakeholding framework can help explain the emergence of cancerous behaviors between humans, and it also may help us better understand cancer itself.[118]

Based on Hamilton's rule, the same individual can display nurturing behaviors toward kin and extractive behaviors toward non-kin. For example, a tyrant may extract from his people but lovingly nurture his own children. The person hasn't changed between these two scenarios. What has changed is the context; specifically, the tyrant's degree of vested interest in the relationships, which affects goal congruence, alignment of interests, and degree of interdependence.

The human body can be considered a society of cells with identical genes. The trillions of cells in a normal body run their algorithms as a coordinated, interdependent superorganism. Cells in the body are known to nurture and behave altruistically toward one another: apoptosis is one example, as is the specialization of cells in a multicellular organism.[119] When the network of intercon-

118. Yun, Joon, Jeremy Yun, and Conrad Yun, Interdependent Capitalism: Redesigning the Social Contract through Inclusive Stakeholding [Kindle edition], February 15, 2019; https://www.amazon.com/Interdependent-Capitalism-Redesigning-Inclusive-Stakeholding-ebook/dp/B07NSW9SYZ.
119. Williams, Sarah, "Researchers Identifies Unusual 'Altruistic' Stem Cell Behavior with Possible Link to Cancer," Stanford Medicine, June 11, 2012, http://med.stanford.edu/news/all-news/2012/06/researcher-identifies-unusual-altruistic-stem-cell-behavior-with-possible-link-to-cancer.html; "Why Evolution Drives Some Cells to Altruism," Phys.org, September 18, 2006, https://phys.org/news/2006-09-evolution-cells-altruism.html.

nected algorithms manifests a mutually vested interest in each other's success, the organism thrives.

Intercellular interdependence, however, appears to decline as we get older, and this may contribute to the aging process.[120] Which processes lead to the loss of intercellular interdependence remains to be determined. Perhaps the loss of a central biological clock after pineal involution promotes dyssynchrony among cells. Maybe a loss of power, control systems, or repair mechanisms also contribute to the loss of intercellular interdependence.

Perhaps the loss of interdependence promotes selfish behavior among cells whereby existing bioalgorithms are subverted to promote extractions. Internalities are externalized, leading to perverse incentives, and competition for resources emerge. Not unlike self-dealing nations, tissues in the body become tribal and extract from the total system. For example, tissues appear to hoard high-density stores of energy such as fat. Indeed, an increasing degree of adiposity is observed in every tissue of the body as we get older.

Consider cancer through this same lens. When normal cells lose intercellular interdependence, they act more independently. Once independence is established, a conflict of interest develops.

Thereafter, evolution can select for more extractive behaviors. Whereas alignment of interests and competition is a race to the top, malalignment of interests and competition is a race to the bottom. Over many divisions of the cancer cell, selection favors the emergence of evermore extractive algorithms that drive the cell to become a self-expanding beast at the expense of the host. The fractal analogies to extractive social, political, and economic institutions are self-evident.

This lens offers a new target for treating cancer: to reestablish interdependence among cells.

One of the conventional theories about how to treat cancer is to attack extractive algorithms in mutant cells. Blocking growth factor pathways is an

---

120. Suma, Daniel, Aylin Acun, Pinar Zorlutuna, and Dervis Can Vural, Interdependence Theory of Tissue Failure: Bulk and Boundary Effects, The Royal Society, February 21, 2018, https://royalsocietypublishing.org/doi/full/10.1098/rsos.171395.

example. This approach, however, may prove futile if intercellular interdependence is not reestablished. Even worse, the treatment can backfire by acting as an evolutionary selector for more aggressive algorithms, the way antibiotics can select for resistance.

We hypothesize that reinserting algorithms of intercellular interdependence may allow all those extractive behaviors to self-domesticate into regulated normal behaviors that serve the host rather than the cancer. Essentially, from the perspective of cancer, the host becomes an externality that cancer pollutes and exploits.

We are early in our thinking about this approach. We wonder about injecting oxytocin into tumors to increase a nurturing tendency among cells, since the hormone is known to promote nurturing behaviors in humans. There is some preliminary data on this idea.[121]

For these reasons, we believe that the biological basis of intercellular interdependence—and the mechanism of its loss in cancer and aging—warrant further investigation.

121. Ji, H., Na Liu, Yingchun Yin, Sinmei Wang et al., Oxytocin Inhibits Ovarian Cancer Metastasis by Repressing the Expression of MMP-2 and VEGF. Journal of Cancer 9, no. 8 (2018):1379-1384, http://www.jcancer.org/v09p1379.htm.

# The Remission

In September 2008, the financial markets witnessed a fortnight like no other. Lehman Brothers toppled into bankruptcy, stock prices were in freefall, and a treasury secretary was brought to bended knee trying to save a teetering global financial system—a *Kayfabe* moment of asking for mercy.

I spent those weeks on the road, listening, watching, and taking notes for posterity. In an age of information overload, it's unclear if future society will remember such events, let alone care about them. Fukushima, anyone?

Observing a gargantuan interconnected system collapsing in slow motion exposed what, to me, were fatal flaws in the modern financial system (cryptocurrencies are poised to exacerbate, not mitigate, these issues).[122] I described the flaws in a series of essays, but I offered no solutions for them.[123] I couldn't think of any.

I don't think the experts could think of any either. I am a physician, and surgeons have a phrase called "peek and shriek"—slang for opening up a patient, realizing that things are far worse inside than they seemed preoperatively, and stitching up without performing any procedure. When there is no cure, we focus on managing the symptoms as compassionately as possible. But let's face it; as doctors, we are just kicking the can down the road before the patient eventually kicks it.

I believe this is what the caretakers of our global financial system did after opening up the patient a decade ago. These fundamental flaws in the system had gone undetected for years, when earlier detection might have offered better

122. Yun, Joon, Cryptoassets Pose Existential Threat to the Financial System, and It's Not in the Way You Might Think [Kindle edition], December 8, 2017, https://www.amazon.com/Cryptoassets-Existential-Threat-Financial-System-ebook/dp/B078DLL4CC.

123. Yun, Joon, Price and Money: Wag the Dog? [Kindle edition], October 8, 2018, https://www.amazon.com/Price-Money-Wag-Joon-Yun-ebook/dp/B07J69FD2F/ —at Goldman Sachs New World Headquarters.

treatment options. Once metastasized and spread everywhere, these issues could no longer be addressed without killing the patient. So, they just stitched up and pumped the patient with various fluids—a.k.a. liquidity—to prop up the numbers for a little while.

During the current heady times, it's easy to be unaware that we still are in this period of "a little while." Instead, most of the world has gone back to kibitzing about who's doing what to whom and wondering what's for dinner. Such is the bliss of remission.

---

One tool of the self-expanding beast is to corner its underlying constituents into a double bind. The self-inflating bubble of the financial system is an example. The rest of this essay is technical in nature, for those inclined to take a deeper technical dive.

First, here are some numbers and definitions.

The total market value of all net worth in the world (hereby designated $W_t$ ) increased in 2018 to approximately \$317 trillion.[124] Meanwhile, the total hard currency in circulation around the world in notes and coins (hereby designated $C_t$ ) is around \$5 trillion.[125]

---

124. For the purposes of this article and for simplicity's sake, we are assuming that net worth is equivalent to all the net assets in the world; see "Why Wealth Matters. The Global Wealth Report," Credit Suisse, 2019, https://www.credit-suisse.com/corporate/en/research/research-institute/global-wealth-report.html; see page 106 of "Global Wealth Databook 2018," Credit Suisse Research Institute, https://www.credit-suisse.com/media/assets/corporate/docs/about-us/research/publications/global-wealth-databook-2018.pdf.
125. For the purposes of this article, we are only counting hard currency and not cash or currency that is held in financial institutions. These latter types of cash or currency are in reality merely liabilities on the balance sheet of financial institutions and not actual cash or currency that can be used or deployed at will. For those of us who were around during the financial crisis of 2008-2009, the cash that we had on deposit at banks was not actually available. I remember hearing about people trying to make a large cash withdrawal at their bank and being told that the withdrawal would be limited to a small fraction of what they wanted. They had to wait up to a week to get the remaining amounts. The bankers also tried to dissuade people from trying to withdraw cash during the crisis for obvious reasons (they didn't have the hard currency immediately available). See page 449 of "Statistics on Payment, Clearing and Settlement Systems in the CPMI Countries: Figures for 2015," Committee on Payments and Market Infrastructures, 2016, https://www.bis.org/cpmi/publ/d152.pdf; https://en.wikipedia.org/wiki/Circulation_(currency); Hartman, Mitchell, "Here's How Much Money There Is in the World—and Why You've Never Heard the Exact Number," Business Insider, November 17, 2017, https://www.businessinsider.com/heres-how-much-money-there-is-in-the-world-2017-10.

## Implied Liquidity Capacity

Let's define the ratio of total hard currency to total net worth (hereby designated $X_{tctw}$) as:

$$X_{tctw} = \frac{C_t}{W_t}$$

Based on approximate data available today:

$$X_{tctw} = \frac{\$5 \; trillion}{\$317 \; trillion} \sim 0.015$$

$X_{tctw}$ can be viewed as the implied liquidity capacity of the global financial system.[126] $X_{tctw}$ closer to zero connotes lower implied liquidity capacity. $X_{tctw}$ closer to 1.0 connotes higher implied liquidity capacity.

## Implied Liquidity Stress

Let's define the ratio of total net worth to total hard currency (hereby designated $X_{tctw}$) as:[127]

$$X_{tctw} = \frac{W_t}{C_t}$$

Based on approximate data available today:

$$X_{tctw} = \frac{\$317 \; trillion}{\$5 \; trillion} \sim 63.4$$

The significance of $X_{tctw}$ is the following. On the one hand, $X_{tctw}$ can be thought of as the implied purchasing power of hard cash. In a way, rising $X_{tctw}$ can be seen as a good thing, since money can buy more—assuming you are holding

126. Implied liquidity capacity of 0.015 can be construed in the following way. In case of a global run on hard currency as people try to trade their net worth for cash, 0.015 is the probability a person gets 100% of their net worth traded for cash. That's akin to being first in line at a bank that is about to become insolvent. Or, 0.015 can be seen as 1.5 cents on the dollar that everyone would recover if everyone were to split the hard currency equally.

127. One can think about net worth as call options on cash (such as checking account) plus assets that could be liquidated in a transaction ultimately for cash.

cash. On the other hand, $X_{tctw}$ can be defined as the implied liquidity stress of global net assets. Rising $X_{tctw}$ connotes rising implied liquidity stress. Implied liquidity stress is the inverse of implied liquidity capacity.

In a situation of global financial crisis, if all holders of global net assets sought immediate liquidity—that is, they wanted to trade all their assets for hard currency—it would create a run on the hard currency. Downward pressure on asset prices could be significant, given that $W_t$ is 63.4-fold larger than $C_t$ .

## *Implied Liquidity Stress Trends from 2005 to 2017*

| Year | Total Net Worth[128] (in USD billions) $W_t$ | Total Notes and Coins in Circulation[129] (in USD billions) $C_t$ | $X_{tctw} = \dfrac{W_t}{C_t}$ |
|---|---|---|---|
| 2005 | 178,955 | 3,111[130] | 57.5 |
| 2006 | 203,672 | 3,467 | 58.7 |
| 2007 | 228,245 | 3,939 | 57.9 |
| 2008 | 206,806 | 4,263 | 48.5 |
| 2009 | 222,701 | 4,574 | 48.7 |
| 2010 | 234,642 | 4,205[131] | 55.8 |
| 2011 | 248,812 | 4,427 | 56.2 |
| 2012 | 262,266 | 4,616 | 56.8 |
| 2013 | 279,241 | 4,661 | 59.9 |

128. See "Statistics on Payment: Figures for 2015," pp. 78-94.x.
129. See "Global Wealth Databook 2018," p. 109.
130. See "Statistics on Payment and Settlement Systems in the CPSS Countries: Figures for 2009," Committee on Payment and Settlement Systems, 2011, p. 413, https://www.bis.org/cpmi/publ/d95.pdf. Applies to data from the years 2005 through 2009.
131. See "Statistics on Payment, Clearing and Settlement Systems in the CPSS Countries: Figures for 2010," Committee on Payment and Settlement Systems, 2012, p. 417, https://www.bis.org/cpmi/publ/d99.pdf. Applies to data from the years 2010 through 2015.

| 2014 | 277,938 | 4,513 | 61.5 |
| 2015 | 275,531 | 4,535 | 60.8 |
| 2016 | 285,257 | 4,686[132] | 60.9 |
| 2017 | 303,126 | 4,831[133] | 62.7[134] |

## Liquidity Under Normal Conditions

Implied liquidity stress is a theoretical concept that captures latent stress in the system. Under typical conditions, however, virtually everyone is willing to sit on their perceived net worth instead of trading it in for hard cash. For example, people who put money into a checking account own the ability to call the hard cash instead of actually sitting on hard cash. Meanwhile, some people are happy to sit on hard cash.

Under typical conditions, the markets are defined by marginal liquidity. The marginal stress of hard cash looking to be traded for assets, and the marginal stress of assets looking to be traded for hard cash, mutually diffuse each other through price discovery. Orderly transactions in a functioning market prevent runs on hard currency.

## Liquidity Under the Stress of Systemic Asset Price Declines

But here is the problem: when the price of assets falls to the point where there is fear they will fall further, the marginal stress of assets looking to be traded for hard cash increases. Meanwhile, holders of hard cash become less eager to trade

---

132. See "Statistics on Payment, Clearing and Settlement Systems in the CPMI Countries: Figures for 2016," 2017, p. 422, https://www.bis.org/cpmi/publ/d172.pdf.
133. See https://stats.bis.org/statx/srs/table/CT2?m=1&p=2017&c=; "Statistics on payment, clearing and settlement systems in the CPMI countries—Figures for 2016," BIS, December 15, 2017, https://www.bis.org/cpmi/publ/d172.htm; UK is listed as NAP in 2017. Over the years, inconsistencies exist in data reporting.
134. Certain periods have seemingly high market liquidity. These periods are generally leading indicators of future global asset price decline. Why? Periods of high market liquidity generally lead to asset price appreciation. Hard currency, however, typically does not rise very much. Thus, the implied liquidity capacity generally declines during periods of high market liquidity. The correction occurs by virtue of contraction of asset prices. Broad asset price declines reduce liquidity in a self-reinforcing fashion.

it for assets. The bid-ask spread for hard cash widens. Liquidity declines and/or prices drop further. These dynamics are self-reinforcing.

Other factors, including margin calls, leverage, credit, momentum, reflexivity, and psychology, can feed into the self-reinforcing relationship between rising marginal liquidity stress and marginal price declines.

## *Liquidity under the Stress of Systemic Asset Price Increases*

Mirror image issues lurk when prices (assets, goods) are rising. Sitting on cash becomes unattractive, given the seeming depreciation of the value of cash. Even sitting on near cash (money market funds or checking accounts) feels unattractive. Thus, the amount of hard cash looking to be traded for assets increases. Everywhere you will see cash chasing returns or looking to be traded for assets. For those looking to raise cash, this era will feel like easy money.

During periods of rising prices, the marginal stress of liquidity typically falls. Other factors, including leverage, momentum, reflexivity, and psychology, can feed into the self-reinforcing relationship between falling marginal liquidity stress and rising marginal price of assets.

As prices rise, the mark-to-market nature of net worth leads to increasing $W_t$, which also increases $X_{tctw} = \dfrac{W_t}{C_t}$, assuming printing of currency has not kept pace.[135]

## *Non-Robustness of the Financial System*

The self-reinforcing phenomena described above reveal the Achilles' heel of the financial system. The envelope in which the financial system remains robust is narrow, and the risk of runaway phenomena lurks not far from the topography of seeming self-stability.

---

135. See Yun, Joon, "Mark to Market: Is an Unrealized Price Gain A Real Asset?" Pensions & Investments, March 23, 2009, https://www.pionline.com/article/20090323/ONLINE/903209993/mark-to-market-is-an-unrealized-price-gain-a-real-asset; "Do Private Returns Produce the Social Returns We Need?" Institute for New Economic Thinking Conference Session, April 9, 2014, https://www.ineteconomics.org/events/human-after-all/agenda/do-private-returns-produce-the-social-returns-we-need.

A system that is robust, until it is not, is a non-robust system. The nature of liquidity is such that the increased or decreased demand for it is self-reinforcing.

As bizarre as it may seem, the reality is that, during bubbles and crashes, as asset prices rise, they are getting *cheaper* relative to the supply of liquidity, and as asset prices fall, they are getting more expensive relative to the supply of liquidity. That's an inherently unstable system.

## *Debasing Assets*

An underappreciated variable in the growth of $W_t$ is the unit volume growth of assets over time. Even if there is only mild inflation of the price of an asset over time, if there are massive increases in the unit volume of that asset, $W_t$ can increase dramatically. By way of analogy, the price of a company's stock can be flat, but if the number of shares issued increases tenfold, then the market capitalization of the company increases tenfold as well.

Here is a concern. Economists and policymakers typically focus on the inflation of unit prices of each asset (which has been mild). This does not address the issue of unit volume growth, however, which contributes to the massive growth of $W_t$ that in turn leads to significant increases in implied liquidity stress.

We have been printing assets—a whole lot of it and for a long time.[136] We have debauched assets far more than we have debauched money. Yet, the reflexive concern among modern economists is to fear the printing of money.[137] While an army of economists understandably guard against the debasement of money, no one guards against the debasement of assets.

According to the theory of microeconomics, the effect of mass-printing assets on price should be self-correcting: as the total unit volume of an asset increases, its price declines. Or, as more types of assets are produced and availability of substitutes increases, the prices of these assets would decline. Therein lies the rub.

---

136. Most people are familiar with the notion of debasing hard cash relative to gold. One can also think about the imbalance of total net worth versus total hard currency as debasing worth relative to hard currency.

137. "There is no subtler, no surer means of overturning the existing basis of society than to debauch the currency," Keynes observed in 1919. See https://en.wikisource.org/wiki/Essays_in_Persuasion/Inflation.

Because the system does not tolerate aggregate decline of asset prices, policymakers are forced to manage the aggregate economy to 2 percent inflation (discussed below), ignoring unit volume growth of assets. This short-term handcuff on policymakers promotes the long-term growth of $W_t$ and $X_{tctw}$.

Thus, the growth of the total units of assets, even in the context of low inflation of price per unit, leads to massive expansion of the size of the total aggregate balance sheet, relative to total hard cash.[138]

## The Double Bind

Here is a fundamental double bind. On the one hand, when a broad price decline of assets leads to contraction of $W_t$ , the marginal liquidity stress increases as people try to convert their assets for hard cash, of which very little actually exists. It's a run on financial intermediaries, a run on hard cash, and a run on liquidity that can only be stopped by government action and psychological weapons. On the other hand, when asset prices rise broadly, it exacerbates implied liquidity stress, which sets up the next major bear market to be even worse.

## Low Inflation Is the Least of All Evils

Of the two outcomes of the double bind, modest asset price inflation, managed through policy and psychology, is widely viewed as the only viable path.

As mentioned above, over time, human endeavor leads to net production of assets, both in terms of unit volume as well as the number of distinctly different assets. Therefore, if total hard cash is stable, the growth of $X_{tctw}$ signals an increase in the deflationary potential of asset prices.

There are many strong arguments, however, for using interventions to prevent actual asset price deflation. Two of them are discussed here.

First, there is an existential argument against allowing broad asset price deflation. Asset price deflation promotes hoarding of hard currency. The inherent value

138. See Adrian, Tobias, and Hyun Shin, "Liquidity and Financial Cycles," BIS Working Papers No. 256, July 2008, https://www.bis.org/publ/work256.pdf ; Yun, "Mark to Market."

of currency as a store of value is predicated on its utility as a medium of exchange. The shifting use of hard cash, from serving as a medium of exchange to a store of value, perversely invalidates its storage value in a self-referential way. If hard cash loses its perceived value, we are back to the barter system of exchange, which was a highly inefficient system of trade that led to the invention of currency in the first place. Hoarding fiat currency as a storage of value is a self-referential fallacy.

Second, there is a practical argument against allowing broad asset price deflation. Sustained deflationary pressure leads to runs on the banks and other financial intermediaries. The deflationary spiral would not get very far before the financial system would freeze and liquidity goes to near zero. "Guns and gold" barter system would emerge quickly once liquidity evaporated. Catastrophic social upheaval would likely ensue.

Feed-forward hyperinflation of asset prices, for reasons described above, is not a viable option.

So, we are left with low inflation of asset prices as the preferred target among policymakers as the least of all evils.

When policymakers manage inflation, however, they need to consider not only the first-order effects their policies have on inflation but their second-order effects on implied deflationary stress associated with implied liquidity stress. The notion that inflation *inherently* increases deflationary risk (by increasing $X_{tctw}$ ), which is a double bind, is not generally recognized.

## Tools

Numerous tools exist to moderate the self-reinforcing forces of asset prices, including printing (or destroying) hard currency, policy, and managing public psychology. On occasion, the reactions to deflationary pressures have been insufficient, leading to global financial crashes such as those that happened in 1929 and 2008. By and large, however, most of these measures do work.

We will have to have some faith that the coordinated policy responses around the world can continue to mitigate risks and steer the world away from financial collapse, as needed. Whether the emergence of cryptocurrencies will mitigate financial system risks or exacerbate them remains to be seen.[139]

## *System Risk Increases as Nations Move Away from Hard Cash to Digital Money*

Printing or destroying hard currency is a policy consideration. On the one hand, too little hard currency $C_t$ exists than would be needed to provide liquidity when everyone runs for the door trying to trade their assets for cash. On the other hand, printing more hard cash is also not a great option because, over time, it will dramatically expand $W_t$ and $X_{tctw}$. This increases the risk and magnitude of downstream crashes.

Overall, however, as $W_t$ continues to increase, a case could be made that $C_t$ should be increased to keep $X_{tctw}$ stable. That is, the amount of hard currency in circulation should be increased.

Instead, the political dynamic is such that many nations are trying to eliminate hard cash and make it criminal to even own it. They are trying to shift the financial system from hard cash to digital cash.

Here's why this trend is a disaster in the making.

The existence of hard cash is what creates an upper limit on money velocity. The hard cash you believe you put in your checking account at the bank has been lent to a small business, and that cash was in turn put into another bank's checking account, etc. At the end of a long string of contracts, someone actually holds that physical cash. The layers between contracts and counterparty risk between you and that physical cash is far more than any one person understands. This is the foundation of bank runs.

Now, imagine a nation that has eliminated all hard cash. The money velocity is no longer limited by someone holding cash at the far end from where it started. In

---

139. See Yun, Cryptoassets.

the world of digital money that we seem to be headed toward, the money becomes circular and money velocity goes to infinity. Runaway forces of expansion and the collapse of financial markets will become far worse than they are now.

Prudence suggests that hard currency should be kept in circulation instead of being replaced by digital currency.

## Depopulation

Managing policy toward asset price inflation has been buttressed by demographic expansion. Demographic contraction looms, however, especially in wealthy countries. The looming demographic contraction is a deflationary force that could reduce aggregate demand.[140]

## Summary of the Liquidity-Price Conundrum

- Few people realize or understand how little hard currency exists, relative to the perceived total net worth of the world.
- During typical scenarios, people are happy not to hold hard cash and are happy to be sitting on the mark-to-market assets on their balance sheet (checking account, car, house, stocks, bonds, collectibles, etc.).
- During episodes when asset owners want to trade an asset for hard cash, the relative scarcity of hard cash leads to price crashes, liquidity freezes, or both.
- Many economists lump near cash with physical cash, which confounds the data.
- If the ratio of total net worth rises relative to total currency, the latter is becoming more valuable, on an implied basis. This issue is apparent to almost no one, except during deflationary spirals when people notice that hard cash is difficult to find.

140. See Yun, Joon, "The Next Black Swan: Global Depopulation," Forbes, December 6, 2012, https://www.forbes.com/sites/joonyun/2012/12/06/the-next-black-swan-global-depopulation/#13cf9ebf5868.

- Cash cannot be perceived by people in the system as scarce and valuable. If that happens, people will hold cash for the storage value. At the end of the day, however, the entire existential proposition of fiat currency is to facilitate exchange (otherwise we are back to the inefficient barter system). Hoarding fiat currency as a store of value is a self-referential fallacy.

- We have guarded against debauching currency but failed to guard against debauching assets.

- The financial system is fraught with self-reinforcing loops of instability, double binds, and existential fallacies.

- The system is generally functional during long periods of complacency, punctuated by panic runs on banks and financial institutions. This lack of system resilience when it is most needed is a fundamental bug in the system.

- The looming demographic contraction is a deflationary force that could reduce aggregate demand.

- The risks of inflation and deflation are known to the Fed. The notion that inflation *inherently* increases deflationary risk (by increasing $X_{tctw}$), which is a double bind, is not generally recognized.

- When policymakers manage inflation, they need to consider not only the first-order effects their policies have on inflation but also their second-order effects on the implied deflationary stress associated with implied liquidity stress.

- The only way to deal with this tautologically flawed system—which some would classify as a Ponzi scheme—through policy is to perpetuate the Ponzi scheme.

- As nations try to eliminate hard cash in favor of electronic cash, money becomes circular and money velocity goes to infinity. Runaway forces of expansion and the collapse of financial markets will become far worse than they are now.

- Prudence suggests that hard currency should be kept in circulation instead of being replaced by digital currency.

# Stewarding
# Future Leaders

Stewardship is defined as the responsibility to shepherd and safeguard the interests of others. Many of us are in positions of stewardship in public corporations, private enterprises, and charitable organizations. Warren Buffett, perhaps the most widely followed business leader of our time, speaks often of the importance of stewardship in business. It is striking, then, to see the dearth of courses discussing the concept of stewardship at top American business schools. In the 2013-2014 online course catalogs of the top five MBA programs in America (as ranked by *U.S.News and World Report*[141]), "stewardship" is nowhere to be found in any course title. To put this into context, each of these schools offered at least five classes with the word "leadership" in the title. In the detailed descriptions of courses offered at the number one ranked business school in the same report, the word "leadership" appears 108 times. The word "stewardship" is not mentioned once. The closest mention of the word appears in the context of how to steward *yourself,* in a course entitled "Leading Your Life."

Indeed, while not all leaders behave this way, the widespread popularization of the words "leader" and "leadership" has insidiously helped perpetuate the abuse of followers by enabling the self-dealing beast to domesticate and redirect the anger of the abused populace toward those marked as "others." Think of every political campaign ever.

That's why, despite more than 50,000 books published with the word "leadership" in the title, the public hungers for the next one.[142] One wonders why, if the

141. See "Best Business Schools," U.S.News and World Report, 2019, https://www.usnews.com/best-graduate-schools/top-business-schools/mba-rankings.
142. https://www.google.com/search?tbo=p&tbm=bks&q=intitle:leadership&num=10.

concept of leadership is so valuable and fundamental, the word was not coined in English until 1821;[143] in fact, the word "leader" has been in common usage only since 1918.[144] Did these concepts not exist before? Hardly. The harsh reality is that these words emerged to serve the leader, not their subjects. The linguistic masquerade enables tyrants to dupe the public and command power at an even higher level in the age of nationalism, globalism, and technology-enabled inter-connectedness.

If leadership is defined as the nurturing of leaders, it is essentially a form of stewardship. The system self-propagates the way ecological succession or the cycle of life does. If leadership, however, is instead defined as the creation of follow-ers—think of Instagram culture—hegemony ensues.

Fortunately, stewardship—the concept, inherited from the kin tribe age, that preceded the concept of leadership—is an innate core trait. It is observed throughout nature, as exemplified by the nurturing instincts of parents and service behaviors among kin. Such behaviors were evolutionarily selected to meet the needs of social species, such as humans, that grouped around closely related members, or at least did so during the long and stable prehistoric age that shaped our selection. It is our nature to nurture, and in the Darwinian calculus, socially altruistic behaviors toward one's kin can enhance one's own evolutionary fitness, or inclusive fitness.

While such behaviors were likely selected and proved beneficial when humans lived among kin-based tribes, in the modern world of easy mobility and accel-erating social dispersal, communities typically develop around diverse, non-kin populations. Many of our factory-setting behaviors, including the degree to which we trust our fiduciaries and agents, are rendered maladaptive in a world of high-relationship liquidity.

Given this evolutionary dislocation, stewardship of non-kin is now a moral choice rather than a naturally adaptive behavior that fits Hamilton's rule. These days, we all too often feel forsaken by those we call leaders. A mere century ago,

143. See Online Etymology Dictionary, https://www.etymonline.com/search?q=leadership.
144. See Online Etymology Dictionary, https://www.etymonline.com/word/leader.

Captain Edward Smith went down with his doomed ship, the RMS *Titanic*. Facing similar situations, the modern captains of *MV Sewol* and *Costa Concordia* abandoned ship, leaving their passengers to a disastrous fate. Although these are isolated incidents, they provoke a sinking feeling about the broader fate of civil society.

As a species, we've collectively set sail toward becoming a diverse, mobile, and global community, and there is no turning back. To meet the social challenges that accompany this new era, it is more vital and urgent than ever to start a meaningful conversation about stewardship. We hope our nation's stewards can *lead* the way in starting this conversation.

# Multidimensional Selection as an Evolutionary Framework

Multilevel selection hypothesis suggests that selection acts not only on individuals, but also simultaneously on multiple levels of biological organization, including cells and groups. We hereby extend that notion to describe multidimensional selection as an evolutionary framework.

Biology has multiple strata including molecular, organelle, cellular, histological, organismal, tribal, species, and ecosystem levels. Each stratum of a hierarchy can be viewed as comprising a collection of one or more "living" units—these units can compete and collaborate horizontally within each stratum.

Collaboration and competition also occur in the vertical dimension *between* the different strata. That the fates between strata are collaboratively aligned is self-evident: the fate of a cell in the body is generally tied to that of the whole body and vice versa. On the other hand, the fates of units in different strata are often not aligned due to interstrata competition.

Here is an example. Apoptosis of a particular cell in the body (self-death) typically helps the strata above (the organism) and the strata below (genes, from an inclusive fitness perspective). Even as its adjacent strata benefit, however, the individual cell is dead.

Here is another example. Diversity in a system tends to reduce its fragility and increase its robustness. The same diversity, however, also tends to increase stress between underlying members of the system. Since the system itself, as well as individual members that comprise the system, are all simultaneously trying to achieve self-stability against stress, the system is vertically competing against the interest of the strata below it (the strata of individual members of the system).

An extension of the multilevel selection hypothesis is the addition of the temporal, fourth dimension. From this thinking emerges a more generalized version of the hypothesis called the multidimensional selection hypothesis, which adds not only the temporal dimension, but also all possible abstracted $n$-dimensions.

Here is a demonstration of the temporal dimension. Traits face differential selection pressure at different temporal scales. Fractional reserve banking may be positively selected during shorter temporal durations (a particular epoch of self-stability) but may engender herd-behavior risk that leads to adverse selection during a longer temporal duration (due to its contribution to system instability).

Another demonstration is the transition of human species from one that was integrated into the ecosystem to one that domesticated the ecosystem. The latter regime has led to the positive selection of many human traits in the context of the past 10,000 years, but those same traits may lead to adverse selection against humans in a 100,000 year scale if we destroy our ecosystem. At any point in time, each trait is "exposed" to the sum of selection pressures—some that favor the trait and some that select against is—at short and long temporal scales as well as every scale in between.

In the case of humans in 2019, the strata of superorganisms is competing and winning, relatively speaking, against the strata of individuals. It is thus that individuals end up working for "the Man," and the "the Man" does the bidding for the superorganism. Interstrata competition has been largely subverted into vertical layers of nested domestication of humans by memetic superorganisms, genetic superorganisms, and institutions.

Through the lens of multidimensional selection, a better horizontal alignment of stakeholding with others, better alignment of stakeholding between vertical layers of biology—between us, the genetic layers below us, and the superorganisms above us—and better alignment of stakeholding across time, including future versions of civilization and ecosystems, is envisioned as a hope for the future.

# About The Authors

**DR. JOON YUN** is President of Palo Alto Investors, LP, a hedge fund founded in 1989. Board certified in radiology, Joon served on the clinical faculty at Stanford. Joon is a trustee of the Salk Institute and was the $2 million founding donor to the National Academy of Medicine Aging and Longevity Grand Challenge. Joon holds a MD from Duke Medical School and a BA from Harvard University. He has been to Burning Man the past 20 years.

**ERIC YUN** is a Director of the Yun Family Foundation.

**CONRAD YUN** has over 20 years of experience as an investor and entrepreneur. Conrad manages a family office with investments across a range of public and private assets, including in numerous startups. Conrad is also Executive Director of the Yun Family Foundation and its affiliate Palo Alto Institute, which are nonprofits sponsoring initiatives in the areas of aging, nutrition, childhood diseases, technology and art. Previously, Conrad worked in the technology sector as an executive and founder of startups in Europe and Asia and also as a corporate lawyer at Cravath, Swaine & Moore. Conrad is a CFA charterholder and holds a JD from University of Chicago Law School and a BA from Harvard University.

*We are grateful for contributions from
Sung Hee Yun, Amanda Yun, Jeremy Yun, and Kimberly Bazar
and special thanks to Dody Riggs*